Southern Writers and the Machine

Worcester Polytechnic Institute Studies in Science, Technology and Culture

Lance Schachterle and Francis C. Lutz
Co-Editors

Vol. 11

PETER LANG
New York • San Francisco • Bern • Baltimore
Frankfurt am Main • Berlin • Wien • Paris

Jeffrey J. Folks

Southern Writers and the Machine

Faulkner to Percy

PETER LANG
New York • San Francisco • Bern • Baltimore
Frankfurt am Main • Berlin • Wien • Paris

Library of Congress Cataloging-in-Publication Data

Folks, Jeffrey J. (Jeffrey Jay)
   Southern writers and the machine : Faulkner to Percy / by Jeffrey J. Folks.
      p. cm. — (Worcester Polytechnic Institute studies in science,
technology and culture ; vol. 11)
   Includes bibliographical references.
      1. American literature—Southern States—History and criticism.
2. Literature and technology—Southern States—History—20th century.
3. American literature—20th century—History and criticism.   4.
Faulkner, William, 1897-1962—Knowledge—Technology.
5. Southern States in literature.   6. Machinery in literature.   I. Title.   II.
Series.
PS261.F65   1993   810.9'975'0904—dc20   92-12061
ISBN 0-8204-1856-0   CIP
ISSN 0897-926X

Die Deutsche Bibliothek-CIP-Einheitsaufnahme

Folks, Jeffrey J.:
Southern writers and the machine: Faulkner to Percy / Jeffrey J. Folks.—
New York; Berlin; Bern; Frankfurt/M.; Paris; Wien: Lang, 1993
   (Worcester Polytechnic Institute studies in science, technology and
culture ; Vol. 11)
      ISBN 0-8204-1856-0
NE: Worcester Polytechnic Institute: Worcester Polytechnic Institute.

COVER DESIGN BY JAMES F. BRISSON.

The paper in this book meets the guidelines for permanence and
durability of the Committee on Production Guidelines for
Book Longevity of the Council on Library Resources.

© Jeffrey J. Folks, 1993

Printed in the United States of America.

To my parents, John and Hazel Folks

Acknowledgements

I am grateful to the many teachers and students of southern literature from whom I have learned. I would especially like to acknowledge the encouragement and direction of Professor James H. Justus of Indiana University and Professor Lewis P. Simpson of Louisiana State University. Professor Carol Christ of the University of California at Berkeley read the chapter on "Allen Tate and the Victorians" and offered useful criticism. My colleagues at Tennessee Wesleyan have engaged me in stimulating discussion of some of the ideas in the book.

I have benefitted from NEH Seminars at Louisiana State and University of California at Berkeley, from two James Still Fellowships administered by the Faculty Scholars Program at the University of Kentucky (formerly the Appalachian College Program) funded in part by the Mellon Foundation, from several short-term Mellon Fellowships at Vanderbilt University, and from a Fulbright Scholarship to Yugoslavia. An NEH Institute on "The Southern Novel and the Southern Community" directed by Louis D. Rubin, Jr. and Joseph Flora proved enormously stimulating at the point when I was completing revision. I am particularly grateful to Professor Lucinda MacKethan for her advice and direction during this Institute. My son, Matthew Allen Folks, shared research stays at Baton Rouge and Berkeley and listened over the years to my reports on southern writers. I am above all grateful to my wife Nance, for her enduring patience and support.

Contents

Chapter 1

Introduction

I intend to study the ways in which southern writers since 1925 have dealt with the rapid modernization of their region, and to trace the ways in which their response to change has contributed to aesthetic theory. At the beginning I wish to advance several assertions about southern writing which will be at the heart of my study.

First, I believe that change itself is the central subject of modern southern literature, perhaps to an even greater extent than it is a major issue in modern literature in general. The rapid transformation of the New South from an agrarian to industrial society could not be ignored, even by those writers who dream nostalgically of a rural past. Coming from a largely agrarian economy in which even agriculture was, up to the Second World War, little mechanized, the effect of the dramatic post-war change was all the greater. However, one should not overlook the fact that pre-war southerners had much contact with modernity, and, as in the case of Allen Tate, could foresee clearly the coming transformation. The most interesting southern writers, I believe, have been those who like Tate have confronted change most authentically, though this "confrontation" may and does take various shapes.

Second, I find that the impact of modernization has been a re-examination by southern writers of their relation to the region and of the significance of a regional basis for writing. As the New South has become more similar to the rest of the nation, southerners have attempted to define some essential differences which distinguish their region from the national identity. As it becomes increasingly difficult to point out the difference between the South and the nation as a whole, southern writers increasingly locate the difference in temperament or spiritual qualities. In the cases of Walker Percy and William Styron, they assert publicly that the differences are disappearing.

Third, I am interested in the southern writer's recognition of working within or writing against an aesthetic tradition that has evolved conventional responses to change. The southern reaction to urbanization and industrialization began to take predictable form even in the nineteenth century as modernization began to affect the region with an infusion of northern capital during Reconstruction and a return of southern enterprise. The booster mentality was so prevalent in the late-nineteenth century writing that the Fugitive movement of the twenties defined itself by contrast with regional boosterism. In the twentieth century a southern cultural criticism, a critique of modernity within and outside the region, has arisen in response to change, and all southern writers working in the middle years of the century have been affected by their awareness of this criticism. The example of Flannery O'Connor comes to mind as one who has found subtle ways of working within and against the traditionalist critique of modernization.

By examining central works of fiction along with essays, reviews, and letters of selected authors, I hope to arrive at a broad sense of the southern author's reaction to change. The authors whom I examine are interested in the phenomenon of the New South both for its own sake, as a cultural direction which affects their lives, and as grist for their fictional mill. In addition, the southern author was concerned to address the expectations of a readership largely outside the South which brought its own conventions to the reading of a "southern" novel. For example, the series of "typical" southern narrators in William Styron's works parody the biases of the general reader, from the description of the grease-stained paunch of lawyer Thomas Gray to the complacent sex-starved revelations of Stingo.

My study will begin with an examination of the conception of technology which southern writers adapted from nineteenth-century American and European writers. The aesthetic of the machine which southerners adopted was in part derived from the Victorians, whose simultaneous fear and awe of the machine has been characterized as the attitude of "technological sublime." For Thomas Carlyle, in particular, the machine was both the servant to man and the force which threatened civilized life. The later response of John Ruskin, who reacted against the evolutionary theory of nature in his essay "The Relationship of Natural Science to Art," attempted to humanize science through an alternative myth of natural development based on literary classification. As Leo Marx demonstrated in *The Machine in the Garden*, a native American tradition of literary response to technology existed by the middle of the nineteenth century. Emerson, Thoreau, and Melville, among others, recorded distinctly American responses conditioned by their conception of the wilderness as a pastoral garden, providentially located in the New World. The effects of the Victorian aesthetic, coupled with the native pastoral tradition, may be traced in the work of early modern southern writers including John Esten Cooke, Thomas Dixon, Jr., Joel Chandler Harris, and Mark Twain. These authors find the power and efficiency of industrial culture inherently appealing, and they imply technological solutions to many problems which the South faced during and after Reconstruction. Mark Twain's ambivalence toward mechanization, fearing the potentially dehumanizing effects of industrialism yet attracted to the promise of wealth and "progress," is more typical of twentieth-century attitudes than we may wish to admit. Early twentieth-century authors such as Ellen Glasgow and George W. Cable mark a transition to a more critical examination of the machine culture, while Charles Chesnutt, in brilliantly ironic stories and novels, raised questions concerning the participation of all southerners in the prosperity which technology might bring.

The novelists who began to write during and after the twenties explored the possibilities of further aesthetic responses to change. While these writers were not always promoting industrialism, the central thrust of their work was often an attempt to come to terms with the modernization which was already well underway and clearly irreversible. For the most part, modern southern writers have been too realistic to attempt to base their aesthetic on a return to the agrarian past. The seductions of modernity, from the home appliances that make life more comfortable to the liberalization of morality that promotes greater tolerance and variety of views, charmed the early twentieth-century southerner along with the rest of the nation. In the case of William Faulkner, for example, one finds a writer apparently more interested in the moral complexities of Temple Drake, a character type that he returned to in half-a-dozen novels, than the stable order exemplified by Miss Jenny DuPre of *Sartoris*. The emancipated woman and the social transformation that she brings about occupied Faulkner's imagination from his first novel until the fifties.

The crisis of traditional culture in conflict with modernity may well be the central theme of the southern novel since the twenties, but I wish to explore the idea that for the southern author, even for the leading intellectuals among the Agrarians, the battle had long ago been decided in favor of modernity. There is plenty of nostalgia for the past, as in the elegiac stanzas of Allen Tate's "Ode to the Confederate Dead" but very little conviction of an actual attempt to return to a pre-industrial order. Whenever the southerner speaks of tradition, it usually involves a largely rhetorical and symbolic discourse or the more corrosive idiom of historicism, an inauthentic summoning of the past for reasons of nostalgia or escape. Gavin Wright discounts the importance of tradition in shaping actual economic decisions in the South: "Again and again in the last half-century, patterns and phenomena that were thought to be so deeply rooted in the southern tradition that they could only evolve over the generations were, in fact, dismantled or transformed with astonishing speed" (15). Upon close examination, the "traditionalism" of southern literature may also be perceived as often rhetorical or conventional, reflecting an automatic need to invoke the past rather than an author's fundamental vision itself. Certainly, there is in southern writing that point at which a still vital traditionalism and an emerging modernity meet, the "crossing of the ways" defined by Allen Tate, but the southern writer is carried along by the engine of change while the traditional South remains, like the South of Quentin Compson's imagination, at best a tormenting memory.

My purpose is to determine in what ways the southern aesthetic for fiction developed in response to the transformation of the New South from a traditional to a modern culture. Each of the novelists with whom I deal has to a certain extent invented a fictional aesthetic shaped by the author's perception of change. The most skillful used conflicting regional myths as the basis for a richly creative literature.

With the mature fiction of Faulkner, and in the major works of Richard Wright and Erkskine Caldwell, the southern perception of technology had hardened into a wasteland image of dehumanizing cities and automatic behavior. In such works as *Sartoris* and *Go Down, Moses* Faulkner implies that mechanization has contributed to the destruction of the natural environment and promoted a breakdown in communal values. The effects of technological change on the rural landscape, the family, and the individual are themes in the novels of Wright and Caldwell also, for the emphasis is on a crisis following the movement of rural innocents to the city. In Wright's *Native Son*, for example, Bigger Thomas finds an illusory escape from authentic existence in the power and speed of Mr. Dalton's dark blue Buick, but he eventually perceives the role of technology in his entrapment: the newspapers, an organized search party, and the mechanism of justice which amounts to "a vast but delicate machine whose wheels would whir no matter what was pitted against them" (342). While Faulkner seems quite pessimistic concerning the immediate outcome of this crisis, he projects the hope that human beings are capable of adapting to change, even as he nostalgically records the decline of aristocratic culture and the loss of the wilderness, conventions of southern traditional culture that Faulkner had treated with ironic reservation from *Soldiers' Pay* on. In Wright's works the "escape" from the South which forms the central action of many of his stories results in an entrance to the urban wasteland which may be less hostile and degrading than the rural South only in the sense that his protagonist gains control of the violent means of tragic choice. Each of these three modernists travels well into the technological wasteland, and each sees little chance of immediate escape.

The southern response to technology is altered in important ways after World War Two. Because the nascent social change of the pre-war years was quickened, first by New Deal policies including the Minimum Wage law and then by substantial military spending in the South, southerners came to view social change as irreversible. As Wright convincingly shows, southern attitudes toward labor and commercial development underwent sweeping changes after 1940, and these economic and social changes brought the South more closely in line with the rest of the nation. Certainly, distinctive southern attitudes remained, but one questions whether, without significant differences in economic conditions and social structure, a distinctive cultural identity can long remain. After the Second World War the issue was no longer whether the South ought to embrace change but how the region might accommodate the changes that had already been set in motion.

It would certainly be a simplification of a writer such as Flannery O'Connor to suggest that social history had "determined" her aesthetic, but on the other hand her work does adapt to change in ways that Faulkner's works do not. In her writing one finds an awareness of the conventionality of much southern response to change and a determination to write in a fully contemporary manner. Her stories begin with the assumption of the technological wasteland as an accomplished fact, a wasteland which is nonetheless the source of humor more than it is of serious criticism. There is absolutely no sense in her writing of a nostalgia for a lost traditional past. Rather, the confrontation of the rural traditionalist with modernity is a moment fraught with the potential for ironic parody that takes dead aim at the insincerity of nostalgia: Mr. Head in "The Artificial Nigger" is O'Connor's typical traditionalist, and he is exposed as one who uses a spurious rhetoric of tradition for selfish or defensive purposes.

The motives of both traditionalists and moderns are suspect in O'Connor's view, yet in terms of her fictional aesthetic modernization and the varying responses to it provide the landscape for her finest comedy. By focusing on her treatment of change, the reader can observe the full accomplishment of her masterful rendering of social reality; few writers have offered such a revealing dissection of a culture in transition. Further, I will suggest that her stories derive much of their effect from the ways in which they make reference to a highly developed regional aesthetic of change. In turn, O'Connor contributes to the development of this aesthetic through her theory of the grotesque, for she was perhaps the first southerner to present mechanization in a convincingly comic mode. Like Eudora Welty, O'Connor removes the treatment of the machine from the wasteland aesthetic by revealing the limitations of technology to affect more central and permanent human concerns.

In southern fiction since 1960 technological change is presented as an irreversible process, indeed as a process that has positioned the South within the mainstream of American life. Southerners point with a certain pride to the growth of their cities and the prestige of southern industries; the election of Jimmy Carter in 1976 seemed to mark the return of the South to a national role in political power. For the contemporary southern novelist, the urban landscape is the "normal" setting, and there is little effort spent decrying the effects of technology. Earlier responses to change are easily parodied in the works of Styron and Percy, while Ernest Gaines, writing of a rural hamlet in Louisiana, implies the disappearance of the agrarian community as a viable way of life. Percy suggests that the typical American suburb may be found in New Orleans as well as Chicago, and he looks for ways to adapt to the "post-industrial" age of service industries and information technology.

Similarly, the fiction of William Styron seems to imply that southerners are neither victims nor opponents of change but, like Stingo in *Sophie's Choice*, participants surviving the transition and meditating on the future. Styron's aesthetic accepts the present and achieves tragic representation by facing the implications of modernity. To the extent that Styron writes a regional aesthetic, it is manifested in a certain doubleness of his narrative voice, a self-parodying Thomas Gray, the small-town lawyer who both prosecutes and defends, distorts and extolls Nat Turner. Nonetheless, it is a fiction that now accepts the inevitability of change. The writing of Ernest Gaines also shows the pressures of modernization as it affects the rural southerner emerging from traditional community. *In My Father's House* examines generational differences toward progress and material success, and it may be read as a critique of the New South.

More recent southern writers such as Alice Walker and Richard Ford have continued to adapt an aesthetic to the pressures of change, but one might ask at what point the impact of technological and social change will cease to be the primary subject for southern fiction. Perhaps it has already begun to seem less important to writers like Richard Ford and Anne Tyler, whose characters have limited ties with an agrarian or even specifically southern past. Others like Bobbie Ann Mason continue to mine the comic tensions of the traditional South in conflict with a seductive present. Typically regional themes populate even the most contemporary southern novels: an ambivalence toward progress, an awareness of past and community, and, paradoxically, an unusual adaptability to change and willingness, even eagerness, for new horizons.

Chapter 2

Honor in Faulkner's Short Fiction

The treatment of the machine in the fiction of William Faulkner reflects the modernist inheritance of a nineteenth-century response to mechanization as both "iron demon" and mechanical savior. The essential features of modernist response were adapted from such Victorian writers as Thomas Carlyle and John Ruskin, although the modernist artists such as Faulkner are writing with a greater degree of self-consciousness and, through radical types of formal experimentation, are compelling an aesthetic response to modernity that necessitates a decisive "resolution" and that also points toward post-modernist conceptions. Certainly, as critics from Walter Slatoff through John T. Irwin have demonstrated, Faulkner's aesthetic projects certain aspects of opposition and polarity that have their source within the author's artistic perception as well as within the cultural incongruities of southern history and of American society in general.

The treatment of mechanization in Faulkner's novels and short stories reflects the author's determination to comprehend these opposing responses to modernity and to arrive at an artistic synthesis that would permit a sense of future growth, and even of cultural rebirth, without glossing over the potentially destructive elements of industrialization. While most of the short stories were written with periodical publication in mind, as a body of work the stories contain fundamentally similar responses to modernization. The stories which

I discuss here may serve as an introduction to the novels and stories that I shall deal with later, for the apparently "traditional" world of "Shingles for the Lord" is paradigmatic of the fragmenting and unstable, though still "comic," vision in such novels as *As I Lay Dying* and *Light in August*, and *The Hamlet*, while the ironic wasteland of "Honor," a world presented as futile, shabby, and yet potentially meaningful in its tragedy, points toward the great artistic successes of *The Sound and the Fury*, *Absalom, Absalom!*, and *Go Down, Moses*. A close examination of "Shingles for the Lord" and "Honor" will uncover a number of the basic polarities in Faulkner's aesthetic response to modernity and will suggest the artistic methods by which he attempted to resolve these opposed elements.

In following chapters I have focused on those novels which most directly represent the machine and the urban landscape of which it is a part. In *Sanctuary* and *Pylon* Faulkner looked directly into the industrial and urban culture of the future; rather than retreat into the traditional world of agrarian manners, Faulkner advanced toward the center of the modern wasteland that he represented as an underworld of lost and hopeless human beings struggling against overwhelming circumstance and on the verge of transformation into inhuman actors, their faces masked, their bodies resembling automatons.

Nonetheless, the fact that such characters as Temple Drake and Roger Schumann struggle to define identities linked to the future, rather than withdrawing comfortably into a more conventional and familiar pre-industrial order, suggests the possibilities of heroism and triumph that Faulkner would later cite in his Nobel Acceptance Speech. Furthermore, the treatment of modernity in *Sanctuary* and *Pylon*, and in short stories such as "Carcassonne" and "Black Music," is closely related to the success of major novels such as *Absalom, Absalom!*, for the character of Thomas Sutpen, the wholly modern, efficient personality, seeking social and psychological order "in a series of ruthless actions and empty, extravagant gestures" (Singal 193), is the culmination of Faulkner's many studies of modern abstraction and fragmentation. Daniel Singal has elaborated the thesis that, underlying the incest metaphor in many of the novels, rested the incapacity of "the three principal modes" of antebellum culture, "backwoods vitality, small-town probity, and Cavalier identity," to coalesce "into a meaningful identity" (192). I wish to suggest that, in a similar way, Faulkner's representation of the modern wasteland is tied to his awareness of the meaningless language of the past. Modernity is threatening, not so much because of the rapid mechanization in and of itself, but because of a failure of consciousness that has its source in the past. Like Allen Tate, whose relationship to Victorian conceptions of mechanization I will later examine, Faulkner perceives the spread of "abstraction," the decline of meaning into rhetoric and the replacement of positive action by "mere words."

At the heart of this decline of language is the loss of a sense of a meaningful social order and community of the sort that, for a nineteenth-century southerner, was connoted most immediately by the concept of "honor." As Wyatt-Brown shows in *Southern Honor* the concept of personal honor was fundamental to the southerner's sense of self- definition and to his image of community. The breakdown of belief in southern honor in Ellen Glasgow's *Barren Ground* or *The Sheltered Life* and in James Branch Cabell's *Jurgen: A Comedy of Justice* is equally apparent in Faulkner's early fiction. The questioning of moral abstractions such as honor and courage, reflecting the psychic devastation of the First World War as well as the inherent inadequacy of these abstractions to describe modern experience, suggested other, more realistic explanations for human motivation. At the same time, the undermining of long-held conventions concerning moral action and responsibility, proved troubling to artists of Faulkner's sensitivity and raised enormous difficulties in terms of aesthetic representation.

With the lapse of honor as a meaningful term in modernist vocabulary both in high literature and popular culture, a vacuum was created which writers attempted to fill in various ways. A common pose was that of the tough guy: the Hemingway stoic in literary art, the hard-boiled detective in the thriller. A female version of the same type was the rebellious young woman in reaction against her family's puritanical restraint or, in an alternative guise, the character of the prostitute.

In Faulkner's early and middle fiction, if not always later, the term "honor" or "man of honor" is often submitted to ironic undercutting. One might speculate that the impact of the Second World War had much to do with the concept's acceptance in his later work, as if the ordeal of Americans in the war had re-established a context in which the word might be meaningfully used. Prior to this time, however, Faulkner's sensibility contains modernist elements of irony, restlessness, and despair, elements that one critic may have underrated in defining Faulkner's morality as "the chivalric code--that ideal of love as devoted service, of honor, of loyalty to the concepts of courtesy, valor, and generosity" which are "his substitute of a social ideal in place of formal Christianity" (Levins 115-16). The reductionism of modernist thinking requires that, while distinctions regarding good and evil may in fact exist and even be recognized, these distinctions may not be hardened within the hierarchies of conventional moral language. Struggling to clear the air of conventional morality, the modernist prefers physical reality to the abstractions of language, as Hemingway implies with his admiration of the bullring, a contest involving the ultimate gesture of death.

In his stories "Shingles for the Lord" and "Honor," William Faulkner represents the ambivalence of modern society toward the traditional concepts of honor, and indeed toward the very usage of such terms as "honor" or "truth" in the modernist vocabulary. Both stories present illusory notions of honor, which are re-examined within the resolution of each story.

In "Shingles for the Lord" Res Grier is convinced that his own honor is more essential than the life of the farm community in which he lives, yet the ending of the story reasserts the "indestructibility, endurability" of a broader order than that of the individual. In "Honor," on the other hand, Faulkner's aviators are deceived into thinking that personal dignity is no longer valid in the context of the modern world. As those who proudly carry the standard of lost honor for the secular industrial culture, the aviators are appropriately rootless and isolated in flight. However, their conviction in the loss of honor appears ultimately as an exaggerated assertion of the self equally suspect with the personal code of the "man of honor."

Within the rural community of independent small farmers depicted in "Shingles for the Lord" the alienating pride which separates Res Grier from his fellow man surfaces initially when Solon Quick and Bookwright, refusing to begin work until Grier arrives, calculate that Grier owes them "six work units." Quick speaks sarcastically, in a voice with which Faulkner must have become increasingly familiar in the thirties, of the "modern ideas about work" that have been "uplifting" society. Ironically, both Solon and Quick and Res Grier are aware of the insubstantial reality of these "modern ideas" when set against the enduring order of the human community, but both men are also aware that the changing economic order is inescapable.

Solon's emphasis on numerical calculation, work units based upon the mechanization of time, represents the intrusion of a modern vision on the rural community of Yoknapatawpha. The rural order continues its spiral toward fragmentation as Solon Quick reveals his motive of trading the six extra work units for Grier's half interest in a prized hunting dog. Although Quick pays Grier two dollars and agrees to work the next morning splitting shingles, Grier outsmarts Quick by riding to Vernon Tull and obtaining his half-interest in the dog. However, Grier's pride is not satisfied until he further returns Quick's humiliation by "besting" him in the trade over the hunting dog. After acquiring "half-interest" in the dog, Grier knows that Solon Quick's two dollar investment will be worthless. Thus, Grier and his son decide to remove the old shingles from the church roof during the night, an act which precipitates the disaster of the fire.

The struggle for self-respect and individual justice in which Grier and Quick are engaged appears to be a repetition of the popular Southwestern Humor tale in which the humble victim turns the tables on an oppressor, ultimately humiliating him before the community. The story form is familiar in American humor and is related to the democratic ideology of the frontier, where the sympathetic depiction of the underdog permeated nineteenth-century American popular fiction. Unlike the frontier tale, however, Faulkner's rural tale uncovers an economic and cultural conflict in which the protagonist is not simply in temporary personal conflict with the community but in which unremediable problems face the community. In "Shingles for the Lord," we sympathize with Grier, applaud when he outsmarts Quick, but finally view his actions in a context which undermines his self-sufficiency while stressing his role as part of the communal order. Unlike the Southwestern Humor tale, Faulkner's story emphasizes the individual's complicated and interconnected status within an evolving modern system. Unlike Sut Lovingood, whose rebellion seems to be rooted in an inability to "fit in" to the social community, Res Grier simply cannot determine the rules for fitting into an evolving modern society.

Though Grier relies on his neighbors in crucial ways, even among the small farmers of Yoknapatawpha the local community is not an alternative to modern self-consciousness, for the community of independent farmers has entered into the competitive, alienated economic order of the modern world. Even the seemingly idyllic MacCallums in *Sartoris* do not escape the divisive influence of modern world history as Buddy MacCallum must conceal the medal he has won in the First World War from his father Virginius, in whose eyes his military service means reconciliation with the Union Army. Elsewhere in Faulkner's mythical county, the weakening of community is apparent in Frenchman's Bend, from which the Snopes clan has emerged with a ruthless knowledge of economic reality, to the town of Jefferson itself, in which, to cite one example, Gail Hightower and Gavin Stevens experience the crucifixion of Joe Christmas resulting from a deterministic process which Faulkner labels "the Player."

Yet within this same process of fate operates a regenerative capacity for individuals, if not for society, which Faulkner offers as an alternative to modern alienation. Falling back upon a classical vision which itself sought a myth of personal renewal whether in

Vergillian pastoral or Horation retreat, at no point does Faulkner convincingly envision a collective regeneration of the larger society. On the contrary, the sliding of collective society toward the apocalyptic is repeatedly shown in his work, and in the survivors themselves may be seen further evidence of the cycle of self-destruction. Nor should this imply that an escape from communal responsibility into Thoreauian self-sufficiency is satisfactory, for the communal ties are understood as fundamental to the human condition.

Before the comic resolution may come about in "Shingles for the Lord" Grier must envision his place alongside his fellows and within time, for his pride is not only an attempt to isolate himself as an individual but also to escape mortality. This is the point of his exchange with Whitfield, after he appears two hours late for his church work. Grier speaks of a distinction between the practical world of human affairs, governed by "time," and the divine realm interested only in "salvation." This distinction would seem to be particularly evident to the small independent farmers of Yoknapatawpha whose economic struggle enforces an immediate awareness of time and money.

Whitfield's thunderous reply enforces the rigid, fundamentalist order of the community in which Grier lives: "He ain't interested in neither! Why should he be, when He owns them both?" Always in tension with the religious view, the frontier realities under which Grier lives dictate a view of time which is linked to his individualistic struggle for survival, but a divine order of spirit and nature beyond the economic system is never forgotten or questioned. This tension between secular and spiritual reality underlies his outrage at being called upon to work the extra half-day. As Grier says: "So I'm to be penalized a half a day of my own time, from my own work that's waiting for me at home right this minute."

The alienating force of modern economics is at work from the start in the small community of independent farmers in which Grier lives, as his emphasis on "my own time" and "my own work" confirms. This view of time as a possession, and as a means to self-sufficiency and power, indirectly contributes to the church fire, as Faulkner describes the Griers' attempting to outreach the limits of human possibility in their haste and efficiency. There is a sardonic humor typical of the frontier in the description of shingles "raining down," with the men's haste finally unhinging the "whole roof" so that the lantern is overset and ignites the debris. In the narrator's voice, which is the voice of Res Grier's son, there is both the pride and optimism of the unbounded frontier, and the chastened experience of the struggling independent farmer.

Grier has never really ascribed to the belief that time, in Whitfield's phrase, "belongs" to God. He has obligated a day's work to the making of shingles for the church because it is his duty and certainly because of community social expectations, but the orientation toward time for Grier, in so far as he is focused on its individualistic value, is little different than for Flem Snopes: it is a means to self-aggrandizement. And yet in the inanimate world itself, Faulkner appears to be saying, resides an implacable measure of time and the human condition, as it seemed "for a whole minute" the lantern which Grier has upset hung in empty space before descending into and igniting the church building. Of the same unhurried order is the baptismal shift, which remained intact in the fire until "at last it went, too, not in a hurry still."

Ultimately Res Grier, as he literally "returns to his senses," is aware of this eternal order of experience, and this broader awareness separates him from Flem Snopes, whose radically individualistic temper is far more destructive than the church fire. The crisis of "Shingles for the Lord" literally removes the protagonist from consciousness, as in his desperate effort to extinguish the church fire Grier knocks a barrel of water against his head and falls next to the burning church. When he regains consciousness, the entire community has gathered, already beginning to plan a church-raising for the following day.

In addition to the physical punishment he has already received, Grier suffers Rev. Whitfield's humiliating pronouncement of exclusion from the community. It is the very question of what constitutes the "powers and capacities of a man" that is the basis for the comic ambiguity of Faulkner's story, for in striving to prove himself "the better man" over Solon Quick, Res Grier has somehow bested himself as well. The frontier ethos of individualism, when carried to the extreme, has wrought "fire and destruction" if not death in the rural order.

The ending offers only a momentary comic resolution to the conflict. Grier's final statement reasserts his unlimited pride in his individual powers, but Faulkner offers a miraculous, if perhaps illusory, reconciliation of Grier's personal honor with the needs of the larger community and with the eternal realm beyond. Grier's final statement, "what a day!", suggests that he will be reunited with his community. Perhaps even the reductive tendency to transform labor into "work units" will be temporarily controlled. Nonetheless, beneath the surface of the comic story, with its engaging surface of frontier competitiveness and good humor, lies a destructive process of increasing alienation and abstraction which Faulkner was simultaneously examining in less comic stories.

If a regenerating spirit has drawn society together, it is in spite of the encroachment of modern economics with its insatiable abstraction of time and its isolation of men as competitive units, elements which threaten to predominate and overwhelm the cosmic order entirely in such novels as *The Sound and the Fury* and *Absalom, Absalom!*. Faulkner's vision encompasses both the tragic fragmentation of modern society and the enduring verities of the heart, which are timeless but locate man within time, which are limiting in their definition of human nature but lead to a wholeness of being. The tension of polarities is evident in the description of the ruined church and of Whitfield's determination to rebuild it. With the community church reduced to "a red and fading core," Grier reveals that he "had hated it at times and feared it at other," the the embers of the church still contain the "indestructibility" and "endurability" which Grier and the other members of his community (and, Faulkner suggests, of all communities) somehow find necessary. This quality of endurance is threatened and temporarily overwhelmed by the bewildering intrusion of the machine and of accompanying social change, but like the embers of Whitfield's church the endurability of what is most human is never lost.

"Honor," one of Faulkner's aviation stories written before 1930, describes even more bluntly than "Shingles for the Lord" the destructive isolation of the individual through modern self-consciousness. While the subject matter and milieu of the stories differ greatly, the central theme is arrived at in a remarkably similar manner. While Res Grier's comic failure involves an excessive belief in his responsibility to self-oriented labor, the aviators and woman in "Honor" believe, with equal ardor, in a fatalistic and self-indulgent alienation from moral responsibility. In both stories the traditional view of the human condition is threatened by an individualistic economic and social philosophy which stresses the potential for unlimited self-fulfillment.

Faulkner's statement at the University of Virginia regarding his aviation stories indicates the extent of alienation which he intended for his doomed pilots: "That they were outside the range of God, not only of respectability, of love, but of God too. That they had escaped the compulsion of accepting a past and a future, that they were--they had no past" (*Faulkner in University* 36). Faulkner's language is carefully chosen, for it suggests that the aviators have not escaped the past itself but the "compulsion of accepting a past," a rejection of man's relationship to God and of the will to live as human beings. As Mildred is described in a central passage "lying on the divan, crying," she is indeed a "modern," an heir of Flaubert's Emma Bovary in her mixture of self-pity and pride, her cowardice and resolution. Interestingly, it is the lack of fortitude, a failure of nerve and endurance, that Faulkner singles out in describing Mildred. Similarly, the lack of persistence and rootedness elsewhere typify the modern in Faulkner's portrayal of aviators.

The story "Honor" traces the encounter of Buck Monaghan and Howard Rogers, former First World War pilots, who perform as aerial stunt men. Victims of the Great War, which taught them a reckless love for aviation, the men find themselves earning a scant living by entertaining small-town audiences that Monaghan scornfully calls "little bugs" and "colored ants." The more significant theme of "Honor," however, has less to do with the immediate plight of aviators after the First World War than it does with the broader modernist rejection of a conventional language for expressing values. As in the later novel *Pylon*, which incorporates certain aspects of it, the story depicts a spiritual wasteland into which the aviators and women who accompany them voluntarily enter and remain. Symbolic flight away from the earth-bound status of human beings is intended, and the airplane itself is an emblem of the speed, power, and mechanization to which the flyers are attracted, and over which they have little control.

As a modernist protagonist Monaghan is well defined: for he is the product of wealth without family heritage, his father uprooted from his native Ireland, the son serving a king not his own, disillusioned with the "goddamn twaddle about glory and gentlemen." If Monaghan is "crucified," as we learn in "Ad Astra," his despair seems to contribute to the salvation of others, for the German prisoner whom Monaghan protects is merely a frightened victim of the war, a cultured, gentle man with a wife and son who speaks of a brotherland, not a fatherland. While he is doomed as an individual, Monaghan's embittered modern consciousness contributes to the preservation of others, making existence within time possible for others while reiterating his own despair with a life which "ended" on August 4, 1914.

The structural pattern in Faulkner's aviation stories is clarified by a comment in "Ad Astra" in which the Indian subadar speaks of the self-destructive pride which has led to Germany's defeat. Everywhere appears the same cycle of self-defeat, followed by new birth and affirmation. Faulkner particularly translates the common knowledge of Germany's defeat to the level of personal struggle as the subadar speaks of a man who "conquers himself" and a woman who bears a child. The divine resides within the human cycle of deafeat and rebirth itself, for it is the human experience itself which is "godhead" and "truth." In Faulkner's vision, even at this early point in his fiction, the regenerative cycle is at the same time sexual and historical, affirmation following upon a self-destruction inherent in all abstract hierarchies, what the anonymous German prisoner refers to as "pride, a word in the mouth," and what Faulkner himself later called the "shibboleth" which separates human beings from one another.

The story "Honor" follows this regenerative pattern for the Rogerses, if not for Monaghan, whose sexual relationship with Mildred is nonetheless a necessary element of the pattern. This relationship deserves careful examination. Clearly, Monaghan finds it important that Mildred is not "one of those long, snake-like women surrounded by ostrich plumes and Woolworth incense, smoking cigarettes on the divan," a sort of poorly done Beardley with which Monaghan is apparently all too familiar. Rather, Mildred seems to lack self-consciousness as she "came in with an apron on over one of these little pale squashy dresses, with flour or something on her arms." Her disenchantment arises not from the boredom of decadence but from the struggle to live with self-respect on Rogers' income as a flyer, an economic reality rather than a moral or spiritual condition. She complains, "Where am I,anyway? What tenement woman hasn't got more than I have?" Rather than Lost Generation characters who have no connection with the past, the Rogerses are actually very much interested in respectability: they are deeply innocent in the sense that they believe in the very possibility of personal dignity in spite of their impoverishment. They share the quintessential American belief that something will turn up if only one perseveres and does one's best.

Mildred's adulterous relationship with Monaghan is only a transferral of her belief in unlimited possibility from economic to sexual levels. Like Tristan and Isolde, the lovers attempt an unsuccessful escape from time and human complexity; love becomes a transferral of secular history into sexuality, as Faulkner's imagery suggests when their lovemaking, which takes place as Rogers entertains the carnival audience, is described as "like gasoline from a broken line blazing up around you." A similar confluence of sexual, economic and temporal themes enters into Faulkner's description of Roger Shumann's airplane in *Pylon*: a machine which has performed so well that the others have "conjoined with it" so as to remain competitive in the air races but cannot stop racing lest they "be overreached and destroyed by their own spawning."

The sexual relationship in "Honor" reflects the ethos of the secular culture with its emphasis on individual power and on self-gratification, qualities evident in Mildred's rationalization of her proposed divorce, especially in the breezy and "reasonable" tone in which she uses to summarize their agreement as "the only sensible thing to do" (*Stories* 557). One suspects that beneath the surface of Mildred's language lies an awareness of an eternal order of loyalty and endurance, that, like Res Grier, Mildred's modernism is partly a defensive masking of a more conventional and even sentimental self. Nonetheless, Mildred is certainly no Everbe Corinthia, and the temper of the early stories is not the nostalgic, comic tone of *The Reivers*.

In "Honor" love has become subject to a rational process of which the purpose is an illusory emancipation from mortality. Faulkner's distaste for the scene in which Mildred announces her decision to divorce comes across strongly in Monaghan's comment that "it was all kind of hot and dirty." After the divorce has been agreed upon, Monaghan is reminded that he is to perform a wing-walking stunt with Rogers the following day. Convinced that Rogers intends to murder him, Monaghan fatalistically carries out the flight,in which he falls from the wing but is rescued by Rogers in mid-air. Monaghan's fall through space, suggesting both the modern isolation of the individual and the Christian fall from grace, ends in a brief moment of unconsciousness, after which Monaghan decides to give up Mildred. His attachment to modern self-consciousness is so intense, however, that even this crisis is pervaded by competitive pride. Monaghan says that he was trying to give Rogers "something he must fail at like he had given me something I failed at" (*Stories* 561).

What precisely has Monaghan "failed at"? Apparently it is the code of honor itself, particularly the honor which is expected between

colleagues and friends but which Monaghan has failed because of Mildred's attraction to him over her husband Rogers. Like Res Grier besting Solon Quick in the trade of a hunting dog, Monaghan is competing with Rogers, who has humiliated him by demonstrating a greater capacity for stoic abnegation in regard to a woman's love. The quality which typifies Faulkner's early moderns is a confusion of roles, for Monaghan acts out both the rootless and amoral modern, unmindful of any order of truth beyond the present, and the more conventional roles of nobility and friendship. Even when Monaghan destroys Mildred's letter, his action seems less than self-sacrificial, for the gesture defines Monaghan's role as a heroic if doomed creature, beyond the community of human love, a modernist hero in a rootless existence who has had "three or four other jobs in a year without sticking." Having asserted his self-sufficiency, his unassailable individualism, Monaghan epitomizes those qualities which "all the dead pilots" of Faulkner's aviation fiction value more than life. Significantly, Monaghan expresses no emotion at the loss of love; his relationship with Mildred had been passionate but not emotional, in contrast with Rogers, who after the proposed divorce is described as "gray-looking, like when you see a man again after a long time and you say, 'Good God, is that Rogers?'"

Faulkner's theme in "Honor" and in "Shingles for the Lord" is clarified further by an examination of the other contexts in his fiction in which the term "honor" is used ironically, as it is in the story "Victory," in which Alec Gray murders the officer responsible for imprisoning him and yet is decorated with military honors for leading a charge against German lines--an act precipitated by the murder itself. In greater complexity the ironies of individual honor are explored in Quentin's monologues in *The Sound and the Fury*. As Olga Vickery points out, Quentin's solution to the crumbling of his ethical scheme "is to make Caddy admit they have committed incest. In this way he hopes to make Compson honor a thing of importance and momentous significance even as he destroys it" (Vickery 38).

Equally ironic is the use of the term in *Go Down, Moses*, where Faulkner ponders the concept in relation to freedom. The Negro farmer from Arkansas who marries Fonsiba considers himself a "man of honor" living in freedom, but almost immediately there follows Issac McCaslin's reflection that "no man is ever free and probably could not bear it if he were." The illusory nature of personal honor, perhaps Faulkner's central theme in the novel, surfaces again in "Delta Autumn" as Roth Edmonds' Negro lover reminds Issac McCaslin that she did not require a promise of marriage from Roth, whose actions have been determined "long before honor I imagine he would have called it told him the time had come to tell me in so many words what his code I suppose he would call it forbid him forever to do."

In the rural farm community as in the town of Jefferson, honor implies personal dignity, independence, and self-aggrandizement of a sort connected with the increasing secularization of reality. Through his imaginative fictional treatment of those who place honor above life, Faulkner arrives at an understanding of those qualities of love and compassion which seem essential to human beings and to their survival. As Frederick Hoffman astutely noted of young Bayard Sartoris, another doomed representative of prideful self-consciousness:

> There is something, after all, that sustains the human condition despite and beyond modern violence, and contrary to legend. Both the intensity of Bayard's courting of violence and the strength of family and tradition are false. *Sartoris* somehow strikes the balance between their kinds of falsehood. (Hoffman 47)

In "Shingles for the Lord" and "Honor" Faulkner developed a similar exploration of human responsibility and modern consciousness. Taken together, the two stories offer an effective dramatization of one of Faulkner's most important themes.

Chapter 3

Faulkner's Doomed Aviators: *Pylon*

The devaluation of moral abstractions as a guide to existence, in tension with a certain nostalgia for the loss of a sense of order and community, can be traced in the major novels as well as in the short fiction of William Faulkner. Crucial to the interpretation of major works such as *Absalom, Absalom!* is a recognition of the ways in which Faulkner had learned to represent the rise of an instrumental and individualistic ethos in contrast with the decline of a system of shared belief. Faulkner's major novels project the same qualities of ambivalent response that I have traced in "Honor" and "Shingles for the Lord." Indeed, in the similarity of subjects and in the evolution of aesthetic strategies to represent modernity, the short fiction may often be considered as "studies" for the major novels that follow.

While *Pylon* may not be among Faulkner's greatest novels, it occupies an important position in the canon of his works, for in its study of a bleak modern landscape of lost community and expediency it anticipates the alienated, efficient world of Thomas Sutpen. William Faulkner's *Pylon* was the culmination of a concern with treating aviation dating back to the author's own pilot training, no matter how abbreviated that experience may have been, and to the publication of four aviation stories, of which the first to appear was "Honor" in 1930. Faulkner had written of aviation as early as 1925, when he produced sketches for the New Orleans *Times-Picayune*. The earliest treatments suggest the utter irreconcilability of art and machine, a suspicion of mechanization that appears to underlie the disastrous yacht trip aboard the *Nausikaa* in Faulkner's second novel *Mosquitoes* (1927). In this novel the inept crew and pseudo-artist passengers find themselves stranded as a result of mechanical failure on Mrs. Maurier's expensive yacht, all the result of a simple propeller pin malfunction.

In reality, a good deal of ambivalence underlies even Faulkner's earliest treatments of mechanism, and increasingly in novels such as *Pylon* the author reached more complicated responses. If Faulkner never abandoned the essentially Victorian sense of the destructive potential of the machine, he also responded to the sense of power and excitement that mechanization and urbanization suggested to his generation. As an artist, Faulkner sought to understand the effect of the machine on human character. Despite his own decidedly small-town upbringing, he repeatedly located stories in urban and eventually suburban settings (in such cities as New Orleans, Chicago, and Memphis). Some sense of awkwardness with urban culture is evident in all of Faulkner's novels: a discomfort with the city, for instance, underlies the tragic ending of *Go Down, Moses* in which the migration of Molly Beauchamp's descendants to the northern cities is symbolized by the Hebrew exodus and exile in Egypt.

Nonetheless, the fact of urbanization, and of a readership little interested in small towns that they associated with backwardness, confronted Faulkner throughout his career. Written between *Light in August* and *Absalom, Absalom!*, *Pylon* is one of several of the non-Yoknapatawpha novels that illuminates the major fiction of the same period, by virtue of its concentration on the machine and the urban setting. With its repeated suggestion of the effects of automobile, airplane, and the city itself on human beings, the novel focuses more thoroughly on the effects of mechanization, which are treated at less length though perhaps more profoundly in the Yoknapatawpha novels.

Pylon conveys the same excitement with the city and with the "new" that one finds in the Memphis sections of *Sanctuary*. The aviators and their common-law wife exist beyond society's moral conventions; they are not tied to the local mores because their lifestyle is transient and their machine itself frees them from conformity to ordinary morality. Like the character of David in "The Kingdom of Heaven" the aviators are essentially "tramps," but also like David they are messiahs exploring and announcing the possibilities of change. Their experimentation is inevitably self-destructive; the aviator is necessarily a tragic figure in Faulkner's mind, not only because of the danger of flight itself but, more to the point, because he or she tests the boundaries of conventional response, and thus performs a service analogous to the writer in relation to the language. Claiming new experience for a rapidly changing culture that retains a tenuous hold on customary identity, the aviators are necessarily alienated from the conventional community, for which their ties to one another are not a suitable replacement. Yet in Faulkner's fiction the aviators and others who stand for exploration of the new serve the established community, which is inescapably declining toward greater sterility and intolerance. While the aviators will be rejected and crucified, they are granted a measure of license by the community which seems unconsciously to understand their contribution and awaits their appearance.

The narrator in *Pylon*, it should be noted, is a displaced member of the rural southern community who has made his way to New Orleans. His orientation reflects the rural traditionalist's suspicion of change, as well as his exaggerated excitement at the social, material, and sexual experimentation of the aviators. From this narrator's perspective, machines are always connected with some form of human exploitation. Machine-made goods are labelled "shoddy" or "cheap," and mass communication is shown deceiving a crowd of mindless listeners with its sensationalistic stories.

Surprisingly, perhaps, Faulkner's aviators are also from rural backgrounds, unsophisticated and essentially traditional midwesterners who are enchanted by aviation and adopt a "modern" lifestyle at odds with their backgrounds. For Faulkner, however, these "doomed" and alienated aviators are tragic heroes, enacting the inevitable defeat resultant on human participation in time and history. Through his own disembodiment, symbolized by his physical "ghostliness," the reporter-narrator identifies with the aviators such as Roger Shumann, whose body disappears from its entombment in Lake Pontchartrain after his ritualized death.

Part of the novel's meaning is conveyed through the many instances in which human beings and machines exchange qualities. The reporter's repeated insistence that the flyers are "not human," that, for instance, they have oil in their veins, places the aviators beyond the human community. The suggestion that airplanes and automobiles possess sentient qualities, that planes copulate in their hangers or that automobiles possess the instincts of race horses, contributes to the impression that modernity is somehow beyond human definition, for it is now machines that are vital and humans who are mechanical to the point of inervation. The stoic humor and instrumental mentality of the mechanic Jinx are qualities that apply to the aviators as well and to their complicated love triangle and their attitudes toward Laverne's son. At least on the surface the entourage of aerial artists are inhuman in their impersonality, instrumentalism, and unsentimentality.

Faulkner's point, however, is not simply that love has become "mechanical" and unsentimental. Faulkner insists on seeing the aviators as tragic heroes, but they are not simply victims of technology that makes them unfeeling and faithless. Unlike T. S. Eliot's clerk and typist in the seduction scene in *The Waste Land*, Faulkner's modern lovers are not merely negative examples of the decline of civilization; they are victims but they also are creative of a new civilization that Faulkner sees as both inevitable and, surprisingly, admirable.

Certainly, for Faulkner the aviators represent the loss of tradition. By and large they have lost belief in and even memory of the classical-Christian heritage which included the values associated with personal honor, chivalry, and noblesse oblige, a heritage Shumann invokes only through a cynical tough-guy pose that points toward Robert Penn Warren's characterization of Jack Burden. In Jiggs the traditional heritage is entirely swept away by a functionalism that Faulkner likes to represent by means of synecdoche: boots for feet, a single hand outlined in a tight pant pocket. When the aviators speak with nostalgia, it is nostalgia for the code of the craftsman, that is, for a method of production that is only somewhat less impersonal than modern mass production. Even Matt Ord, who speaks as the exemplar of craftsmanship, flies machines which are at best modifications of standard mass-production models. Ord has no real sense of an alternative to his technological society, as is suggested by the fact that his best efforts cannot safely modify the plane which Shumann rides to his death.

Whatever new civilization emerges, it must come out of the sacrifice of the aviators who test not only the latest technology but also the mores and codes of behavior associated with it. All physical processes take on the sense of an unsubstantial, illusory imitation of past "reality," since the future reality has not yet emerged with its own identity. The representation of the human figure in the novel draws on experiments in futurist art of which Faulkner, having lived in Paris in the twenties and maintaining his interest in French culture, would certainly have been aware. The futurist experiment of Giorgio de Chirico in substituting the mannequin for human figures is several times alluded to, as is the futurist interest in the automaton and other machines that mimic human beings. (In his "metaphysical painting" of the teens and twenties, De Chirico used mannequins such as tailors' dummies or robots lacking eyes in such works as "The Enigma of Fatality" and "The Dream of the Poet.")

Deprived of sleep and surviving on alcohol, the nameless reporter, whose grotesquely fleshless frame implies both illness and transcendence, becomes increasingly mechanical. On the second day of the air races the reporter's response to the automaton-like service of diner food, itself a reversal of the rural southerner's delight in home-cooked meals, connects him with the victimization of the aviators. Unlike home-cooked meals, the diner food is dished up rudely by a hand "with vicious coral nails" which looks as if it had been "baked" in some centralized kitchen factory." The pastry is perfectly rectangular, shaped in "scrolled squares," and the entire meal affects the reporter with physical revulsion (*Pylon* 143).

The reporter's point of view is alien to the city with its impersonal diner and the food which has been mass-produced in the city and trucked out to the point of sale. The reporter, like the aviators, is at heart a rural traditionalist, out of his element in New Orleans. Paradoxically, the traditionalist is most conscious of change and most victimized by it, and the traditionalist, in a sense the most inquisitive explorer of the very change that destroys him, is doomed as the scapegoat of progress whose death will eventually formulate the new civilization for the survivors.

This process of death and creation is also reflected in the treatment of art in *Pylon*. The unpleasant character of Jug, the photographer whom Hagood sends to cover the air races, is again a victim of technology. The camera is apparently unconcerned for human life, producing a "cynical" form of art without pity for the human tragedies it records. The distastefulness of photography is mirrored by Faulkner's description of the photographer, whose demeanor may result from "the bilious aspect" of reality as viewed from behind "a hooded lens" and which is developed in the darkness in "stinking trays in a celibate and stygian cell lighted by a red lamp" (231). As compared with painting, photography is seen as mechanical and diminuative, and as practiced by Jug its appeal is to the violent and sensationalistic tastes of an urban mass. Clearly, however, Faulkner recognizes that the more representational and "mechanical" art is emerging and, as his admiration for the novels of John Dos Passos indicates, he was interested in the possibilities of photographic effects in fiction.

The city of New Orleans, especially during Mardi Gras, reflects the structural motif of death and rebirth that, in a broader sense, is applied to the transformation from rural to urban cultures. As with the novel as a whole, the city is depicted at the particular moment of death preceding rebirth, the "death" that follows the exhaustion of Mardi Gras and the beginning of the season of Lent. New Orleans of the twenties, as Faulkner depicts it, is not a modern urban center, but rather a "spent" and "supine" place which the phrase "clatterflaque Nilebarge" associates with a funeral. An interesting description of the city, with its palms and broomsage elevated "out of an old country thought" locates the point of view again in a rural narrator who feels misplaced in "the garblement which was the city" (209).

To this rural narrator, the skeletally thin reporter who finds himself rootless and desperate in the city, traditional moral decisions, once based on the conventions of shared ethics, have come to seem as mechanical and accidental as the city itself. On the level of comic grotesque, the mechanic Jiggs represents this loss of morality in the scene in which, the morning after his drinking bout with the reporter, he considers the "ethics" of returning to steal his friend's whiskey. Paralyzed by indecision, Jiggs stands "immobile," like the "dummy figures" in front of shabby stores and pawnshops. The image of the mannequin associates Jiggs with the modern, and quite possibly in Faulkner's mind with a specific motif of modern art. Certainly the unconscious and fragmented qualities of his consciousness, full of "dubious tagends of plans and alternatives," connect Jiggs with modernist art and poetry (*Pylon* 126).

When Jiggs does decide to reverse his direction and return to the reporter's apartment for the whiskey, Faulkner invokes an interesting metaphor to describe his moral state: "It was as though the entire stable world across which he hurried from temptation. . . had reversed ends" (120). The metaphor suggests a sense of cosmic upheaval to explain the "mindless" reversal of Jiggs' direction, but, because of its association with the trivial act of stealing whiskey, the "cosmic reversal" is undercut by irony.

One of the symbolic motifs of the novel emerges from the title. A marker anchored in the earth, the pylon is the goal for a race in which the airplanes circle near the ground, never close to their potential of attaining freedom from convention. The entire landscape of New Valois echoes this language: the city is low, sunk beneath sea level, so that the dead must be buried above ground. Streets strike the visitor as being maze-like, enclosed areas, through which one travels without noticing the sky. Only briefly do the aviators glimpse the heavens above their machines, or when once the mob of angry

Kansas spectators gaze in shocked indignation at the partially clothed Laverne descending as the victim of their repressed lust.

The stature of Jiggs in contrast with the reporter's height continues the symbolism: the short mechanic whose concern is boots, an article which attaches him to the earth. The reporter is a tall poet manque, attempting to paint the epic of old times on the modern canvas of mechanization and moral instability. His instinct is to compare the machine with horses and aviators with horsemen, but he finds that the aviators, despite their courage, are doomed by circumstances which include shoddy standardized production and the public's demeaning taste for spectacle.

The public taste is satisfied with cheap performances rather than perfection, and the public in fact is attracted to the morbid aura of death that results from the inability of the aviator-artists to find the financial support which they require. Written during William Faulkner's stay in Hollywood, the novel employs film as a simile for the mechanization of taste that he also represents by way of the air races. The association of the flyers with film comics deflates the very real heroism of early aviation. The parachute jumper sitting on an airplane wing with a sack of flour, for instance, "looked exactly like the comedy young bachelor caught by his girl while holding a strange infant on a street corner" (36). His "bleak humorless face" reminds the reader of Buster Keaton and other deadpan comic, whose silent film antics included dangerous stunts involving automobiles, trains, airplanes, skyscapers, explosives, and other mechanical effects. The cheapness of film pervades the description of the aviators' troupe, as Laverne has "harlow-colored hair that they would pay her money for in Hollywood" (44). Walking the streets of New Valois, the reporter and Jiggs "resembled the tall and the short man of the orthodox and unfailing comic team" (56). Even the home of Roger Shumann's father has become a "bungalow," the sort of architecture "which California moving picture films have scattered across North America as if the celluloid carried germs" (304). Along with its shoddiness, film suggests transience, an appeal to the taste of the moment rather than the apparent timelessness of past epic.

At the center of the thematic purpose is Faulkner's representation of time in relation to mechanization. In the minds of the aviators time is measured in hours of flying time (the reporter comically fancies himself something of a pilot with "one hour" of instruction under Matt Ord). A traditional view of time, measured in generations, has been replaced by "terrific motion" which Faulkner describes as "not speed and not progress" (216-17). The aviators are doomed by their loss of time and their attraction to motion. On the speeding automobile trip from Ord's hanger to Feinman airport, the reporter also loses consciousness of "the sheer inertia of dimension, space, distance" (217). In this respect that they are without a sense of settled space, the flyers are compared to immigrants. Even their machines are subject to the destructiveness of change, for the latest airplanes become obsolete after two years, just as the reporter's "news" is read and discarded daily. Hagood comments on the reporter's "instinct for events" but also points out that he "never seem[s] to bring back anything but information" (42), implying that he has lost historical and moral context.

Surprisingly, perhaps, the transience, shoddiness, and fragmentation of the aviators' lives are redeemed at the moment when speed is pushed to its limits during the Vaughn Trophy race. Nearing the moment of disintegration, the flyers achieve a timeless and motionless quality which is summoned in very different terms than the cheap and transient features noted earlier. The four planes resemble dragonflies, and they are pictured "in various distancesoftened shades of pastel against the ineffable blue" (233), colors that dignify the machines by connecting them with the ancient symbolism of spirit and eternity. Even the roar of racing engines is mitigated by distance and resembles music.

The structural pattern, which relies on the transformation of failure at the last moment into a victory that somehow illuminates the future, is typical of Faulkner's response to modernity. Viewing the machine as more or less the Victorian "iron demon," approaching it with all the hesitation and suspicion of the rural traditionalist, the Faulknerian narrator, initially seduced by the glamour and freedom of modernity, eventually observing and reporting sympathetically, earns a deeper insight: the narrator finds that universal human motives, a Promethean creativity and an instinct for exploration and security, underlie technological progress. What was first viewed as a distinctly modern phenomenon is now admitted as timeless and even courageous, the human struggle against circumstance.

Thus, in *Pylon* as the pilots challenge the world speed record with Shumann nearing the point of death, the "mechanical" quality of flight is diminished and the aviator is set against the "ineffable blue," the engines sounding like the soft music of a harp, images that dignify the pilots and suggest qualities of classical-Christian myth. As Donald Torchiana and Edward Guereschi have both suggested, Faulkner's ultimate intention is to present the aviators as heroic and sacrificial.

The consciousness of the tall reporter repeats and enforces the ritual pattern: having forgone sleep and food for two days, the reporter senses on the third day that his body is about to "fly apart" as the time of the air race approaches. A psychic double of the pilots, the reporter is reintegrated to health at the conclusion of the races, at which time, reintegrating the cultural and instinctual levels, he reaches back to his "instinctual" nature, even waking without the mechanism of an alarm clock. Empathetically entering the minds of the aviators in order to report to an debased but apathetic public interested only in the spectacle of death, the reporter also resembles the flyers in his love of art, in the "outmoded" sense of himself as a writer rather than a journalist, just as the pilots are "craftsmen" rather than "laborers" (as evidenced by their strike against the organizers of the airshow, an action motivated by principle rather than money).

Among the most contemporary of Faulkner's novels in subject matter, *Pylon* affords a particularly direct insight into the author's aesthetic approaches to technology. Clearly Faulkner's interest in mechanization began with a degree of rejection that resembled the Victorian fear of the machine. However, Faulkner was capable of seeing the machine as the product of universal human striving for knowledge and achievement. An avid though apparently less than expert flyer himself, Faulkner was obviously attracted to the excitement and beauty of aviation. At the same time that he was nostalgic for the agrarian life, Faulkner could look ahead to the mechanized and urban South, a future that was ultimately shaped by the same universal human compulsions as the past. Coming at the point of transition between the agrarian and industrial South, Faulkner presented Roger Shumann in *Pylon*, Joe Christmas in *Light in August*, and Temple Drake in *Sanctuary* as tragic characters, testing the boundaries of modernity and redefining social, ethnic, and sexual identity. Such heroes are victims of the very public that will later accept with complacency the very changes that their testing has instituted.

Chapter 4

Temple Drake as Modernist Heroine

To some extent, all the female protagonists in William Faulkner's earlier novels are sketched at the "crossing of the ways," Allen Tate's phrase for the point at which southern literary culture encountered the more sophisticated tradition of European letters (*Essays* 281). The contrasting pairs of women in each of the novels that preceded *Sanctuary* group women of rural background with more sophisticated, middle- class, urban women. Cecily Saunders and Margaret Powers in *Soldiers' Pay*, Patricia Robyn and Jenny Steinbauer in *Mosquitoes*, Caddy Compson and Dilsey in *The Sound and the Fury* are examples of the tendency to contrast modern and traditional women. However, the central figure in Faulkner's effort to come to terms with the effects of modernity on women is the character of Temple Drake, for in no other figure does Faulkner so fully dramatize the elements of self- creation and flight from masculine authority that he associated with women and modern culture.

Like Emma Bovary, Gustave Flaubert's tragic heroine of modernity, Temple Drake maneuvers between cultures without the backing of familiar codes of conduct. Faulkner intends a comparison between the two heroines, for early in *Sanctuary* he invokes the memory of Emma Bovary's career as he compares Popeye's smell to "that black stuff that ran out of Bovary's mouth and down her bridal veil when they raised her head" (6). Horace Benbow possesses the training in modernist literary culture which ought to prepare him to interpret

Temple Drake's psychic suicide, but ironically, though his mind resonates with the proper references to modernist culture, Benbow is incapable of empathy for Temple because of his own resentment of women: what else could the reader expect from a sexually wounded "shrimp-carrier" who at one point comments, "nature is 'she' and Progress is 'he'" (16).

Indeed, few critics of *Sanctuary* have been at all sympathetic to its adolescent heroine, although recent commentators have shown more sympathy than did such early critics as William Van O'Connor or Cleanth Brooks, who viewed the novel as reflecting the dichotomy between "traditional society" and "a modern world in which amoral power is almost nakedly present" (Brooks 116). On the other hand, Richard P. Adams sees Temple and Horace as equally inhabiting the fallen world as indicated by reference to the myths of Eden, Persephone, and the Grail Quest. Brooks's view, however, is echoed in a number of more recent discussions, including that of Sally R. Page, who describes Temple as "the young virgin" who is "totally corrupted" (72). In the criticism of Elizabeth Kerr, Temple is a source of "evil" (94), while Ellen Douglas reads *Sanctuary* as the product of Faulkner's belief that "all white women of child-bearing age" are evil (162). Judith Wittenberg finds Temple "the most depraved of the gallery of nubile women that Faulkner created, beginning with Cecily Saunders" (100). More recently, John Pilkington writes of the novel that "so heavily weighted is the relationship between evil and women that some readers have held that Faulkner bore a grudge against women" (122).

Michael Millgate finds Faulkner's negative portrayal of Temple an index of her class: the novel is "the other side of the world of *Sartoris*, a deliberate undercutting of the middle-class and agrarian values which the earlier novel had appeared to offer as positives" (96). More sympathetic is the appraisal of Linda Wagner, who partially excuses the "irresponsibility" of Temple's testimony at Lee Goodwin's trial as a response to her own position as a woman in a culture where women are denied self-determination. Wagner recognizes that in *Requiem for a Nun* only Temple tries to break free of the rhetoric with which the male characters condemn Nancy Mannigoe. In the most detailed and positive of recent analyses, Noel Polk lists Temple's motives in *Requiem* as an attempt to protect her husband and surviving son, an effort to save Nancy's life, and, only lastly, a struggle to restore her own spiritual peace. Unlike Gavin Stevens and Nancy, who live in the past and the future, respectively, Temple lives fully in the present; only Temple confronts change with courage (130ff). In *Requiem*, at least, Polk views Temple as the best representative of moral responsibility.

Critical discussion of *Sanctuary* as a reflection of the effect of modernity on the role of women follows closely along the lines of individual attitudes toward Temple Drake. O'Connor views the mechanized world as a category of evil in Faulkner's writing, while Brooks describes modernity itself as "amoral" (116). In another early assessment, Irving Howe finds that "Faulkner is so possessed by his hatred for the world of Popeye that it is precisely his moral sensibility, outraged and baffled, which prompts his wish to shock" (193), a view that contradicts Faulkner's own later remark that "only by coincidence" was Popeye "a symbol of evil in modern society": rather he was "another lost human being" (*Faulkner in the University* 74). With Richard P. Adams critics began to see that acceptance of change may actually be an index of humanity in Faulkner's novels. As Adams writes of Horace Benbow, "In a fallen world, the attempt to avoid evil does not make a man more than human, but less" (64). Similarly, Linda Wagner finds the traditional world of Yoknapatawpha wanting for the loss of self-determination it forces on women (134), as does Arthur F. Kinney (186ff). The only thorough analysis to focus sympathetically on the relationship of Temple Drake to modernity is that of Noel Polk, whose reading, focusing on *Requiem for a Nun*, documents many original insights while building on the criticism of Adams and Millgate.

That one has seen Temple Drake in earlier Faulkner heroines should be apparent to most readers. Cecily Saunders of *Soldiers' Pay* anticipates her flightiness, the sexually irresponsible side of her nature which seems to betray Red to Popeye. The epicene attractiveness of Temple, whom the narrator describes as seventeen but looking eight or ten (*Sanctuary* 81), repeats elements of Patricia Robyn in *Mosquitoes*, while the suggestion of sexual promiscuity reminds one of Caddy Compson. Temple's passivity, her frequent sense of being a mechanical automaton, repeats elements associated with many early characters in the fiction, from the victimized Dewey Dell of *As I Lay Dying* to the nameless reporter of *Pylon*. Nonetheless, it is in *Sanctuary* that one receives the clearest artistic rendering of the effects of modernity on women.

From her first appearance, Temple Drake is paired with women of more conventional backgrounds, and she is surrounded with men whose assumptions about women were fostered in rural folkways. As Ellen Douglas describes it, in the traditional order "women can impinge on the world and on men only through their sexuality" (163). With the portrayal of Ruby Lamar, we have enough to understand the pressure of the conventional assumptions. Despite her transient existence supported by occasional prostitution, Ruby is paired with Lee Goodwin in the most conventional of arrangements. She is shown cooking and serving food to men, assessing her work "with that veiled look with which women make a final survey of a table" (11). Later, she is shown caring for her sleeping infant and commenting that Horace Benbow "doesn't eat right" (18). Moreover, the harshness of Ruby's opinion of Temple reflects her mistrust and resentment of the latter's freedom.

As we see, even the world of the bootlegger is overwhelmingly traditional when it comes to sexual relationships. Tommy assumes that Temple and Gowan are married because they travel together in an automobile. Lee Goodwin, apparently fascinated by the epicene quality of his visitor, is accused of infidelity by Ruby, to whom he protests his innocence. Only Temple stands out against the traditional sexual code, but at seventeen she is largely unconscious of the Promethean role she will enact.

Earlier in the novel Faulkner introduces the motifs of mask and robot to establish Temple's identity as modernist heroine. These motifs suggest the difficulty of crossing cultural borders, for the effects of such a passage are fright and de-personalization. Significantly, Temple's eyes are "like holes in one of these masks" (194), connoting the stylized acting of Greek drama where broad gesture rather than particular expression is employed. As she rides in Popeye's car immediately after the rape, Temple's face is "like a small, dead-colored mask drawn past [Ruby] and then away" (123). Indeed, Temple's very quality of movement gradually takes on the dignity of Greek tragedy. Her movements, flighty and impetuous at the beginning, become "jerky" and nervous in the Memphis bordello, but by the end of the novel she has gained the grace of marble statuary to which she is compared, sitting "sullen and discontented and sad" in the Luxembourg Gardens among "the dead tranquil queens in stained marble" (380).

The automaton motif also stresses Temple's impersonality, a rigidity that again reflects the difficulty of her transition to modernity. The foreboding of rape triggers a sense of helplessness as she is trapped in the barn on the Old Frenchman's Place. With Popeye, Temple resembles one robot embraced by another as "his hand closed upon the back of her neck, his fingers like steel, yet cold and light as aluminum" (281). Even her love-making to Red is mechanical and inhuman, as Temple is shown "murmuring to him in parrotlike underworld epithet, the saliva running pale over her bloodless lips" (288). In Temple's account of the rape, the sexual act itself makes little impression. Instead, she is the actress holding "the center of the stage" (258-59), more concerned with the dramatic role she plays than with the harm to which she is subjected. Temple becomes the necessary rebel in Faulkner's fiction if his depiction of women is to progress beyond the easy, conventional model to which the rural population is tied. The mechanical aspects of Temple's characterization are connected with Faulkner's conception of her as a heroine of "civilization," a Promethean figure, as is the legendary Cecelia Farmer of *Requiem for a Nun*. Like Cecilia, Temple resists the temptation toward escape or dishonest accomodation with her society, holding out in vigilant apprehension of the modern world as it actually exists.

The automaton imagery is also appropriate to Temple's descent into the urban underworld where she is ferried about in closed gangster cars by her Plutus-abductor and where she resides in luxurious boredom among the consumer goods of the industrial culture. Temple's transition to urban sophisticate is registered by the superficial imagery of gin and cigarettes, of a woman lying in bed or primping before the mirror in new clothes. More significantly, she enacts the modernist woman's loneliness and vulnerability in the midst of a culture that, though modern in its economic and technological tendencies, remains hostile toward the central modernist value of self-creation.

In comic parody of Temple's stately journey through the underworld, Virgil and Fonzo arrive at Miss Reba's establishment as country boys ready to taste the sins of the big city, but through their country naif's account of the whorehouse (they are incapable of perceiving the "nice" women at Miss Reba's as anything but maternal or virginal) the values of pre-modern society are reiterated. The presence of these bumpkins also tends to expose the conventionality of the sexual folkways among the women at the bordello. Faulkner's prostitutes, while seemingly exiled from respectable society, actually constitute the staunchest defenders of conventional moral order. Despite her profession, Miss Everbe Corinthia harbors the dream of a home and family, and the temporary denial of this dream only expands her capacity for maternal tenderness, as the reader of *The Reivers* later discovers. In return for their loyalty to a conservative model of sexual conduct, the prostitutes in *Sanctuary* are nostalgically enshrined by the male rural community, for in their frank acceptance of traditional masculine assumptions concerning sexuality, the prostitutes project the image of a comfortable haven for male self-conception denied or at least obscured by the newer, more sophisticated ethos of middle-class urban respectability.

In contrast to the women and men around her, Temple Drake is self-creative. Despite an otherwise negative appraisal, Sally Page recognizes that Temple suggests "life's potential for creativity and fulfillment" (72). Like the Parisian statuary at the end of the novel,

Temple is ultimately tragic and inscrutable, her nervous adolescence settling into the pattern of ancient suffering. The imagery of modern machine-culture associated with Temple undergoes imaginative re-creation in the course of the novel until the experience of her suffering begins to define woman's transition to modernity in terms of the universal figure of the martyr: she is a Prometheus in conflict with the gods who would hold society to a static, destructive conventionality. Temple's instinct toward self-creation is a necessary motive of adaptation in a rapidly evolving technological culture. What Judith Wittenberg recognizes as Temple's "subconscious desire to be violated" (101) may reflect something other than the private corruption that so many readers have ascribed to her; rather, Temple's violation evidences Faulkner's understanding that all growth requires change, and change implies an unsettling violence, a violation of private security. As Noel Polk explains, "change is in Faulkner necessary to life, though change is not always necessarily 'progress.' But even when it is progress, change makes things obsolete and entails the destruction of what preceded" (42). In contrast to Temple's openness toward change, the pioneering families of Jefferson recounted in the Prologues of *Requiem for a Nun* moved westward to escape civilization, not by virtue of a spirit of adventure but "because of their inability to adapt to the changing world" (105).

The incapacity for change of Narcissa Benbow Sartoris, indicated not only by the imagery of stasis but by her refusal to permit Ruby Lamar and her infant to stay in her and Horace's house, re-enforces the difficulty of change for women in the society of Jefferson. Ruby Lamar enacts the opposite but equally conventional role of the woman who has "slaved" for a "good man," dropping her pretense of respectability but apparently enjoying the masochistic overtones of the relationship. "'I've been in the dirt for him,'" Ruby boasts to Temple, just as later she recounts her prostitution and the beatings connected with her effort to free Goodwin from military prison. However, to some extent Narcissa's and Ruby's gestures of conventionality, along with the maudlin sentimentality of Miss Reba and the adolescent experimentation of Little Belle, serve equally to underline the tensions involved in Temple's more overt rebellion. Whether they cling with exaggerated zeal to tradition or follow Temple in transition toward modernity, the women of *Sanctuary* are all subject to the pressures of change.

As the woman at the crossing of the ways, Temple Drake is the necessary martyr in Faulkner's fiction, permitting the author's imagination to accomplish an aesthetic leap toward a satisfactory portrayal of modern women. Contrary to Irving Howe's impression that Faulkner maintains a "fastidious distance from his material, an unwillingness to breathe the foul air of Temple and Popeye" (194), Faulkner's fascination with Temple, and with a succession of women like her in novels from *Soldiers' Pay* through *The Wild Palms*, indicates the extent of this aesthetic disturbance. The necessity of Temple's martyrdom is made more explicit in the sequel to *Sanctuary*, the novel-play *Requiem for a Nun*, in which the suburban setting accomplishes the prophecy of *Sanctuary* by its distorting the modernist ethos of self-creation to the bourgeois grotesques of consumerism and solipsism. The authorial critique of "progress" is carried on throughout the novel, while the main action, Nancy Mannigoe's infanticide and Temple's pleadings to the Governor to save Nancy's life, is an effort to resist the psychic fragmentation which the parents' divorce would entail. Aesthetically, however, *Requiem* is not an "essay" against modernity but the culmination of Faulkner's need to embrace it; the martyrdom of Nancy Mannigoe and Temple Drake is an aesthetic resolution of the disturbance to Faulkner's imagination that was brought about by the transition to modernity.

If Temple's face wore the expressionless mask in *Sanctuary*, the sequel pictures her having assumed the role of priestess to modernism, the socially ascendant member of the country-club set with the town of Jefferson now integrated into "one vast single net of commerce." The development of America into a model of commercial prosperity fulfills the Edenic vision of the nation's founders as a land of endless opportunity where not even labor is necessary for life. Prosperity is "a beneficence as are sunlight and rain are, inalienable and immutable" (*Requiem* 18). The tone in this passage is almost bitterly ironic, with Faulkner looking back at twenty years not only of personal trial but of national ordeal. Understandably, the matter of Alex Holston's lock, brought to the wilderness from the Carolinas, symbolizes the necessity of limitation, as Noel Polk has well observed, upon the boundless dreams of humanity. Like the image of the prison in Hawthorne's Salem, Alex Holston's lock is an embodiment of necessity, the familiar Old World qualification of human freedom intruding on the New World's dream of unfettered possibility.

Likewise, Temple's suffering forces a recognition of the limitation of Edenic hopes, whether these hopes are founded on the nostalgic impulse to re-capture a lost Golden Age or the futuristic design of a New World. Ultimately the realist in spite of her youthful rebellious curiosity, Temple is the self-creative artist whose artistry has accomplished the painful birth of a new society only to find herself left with the unbearable stasis of self- fulfillment. Temple's originality entails conflict, for as Linda Wagner writes, "only Temple tries to shake loose from the rhetoric [of the male characters, especially Gavin and Gowen Stevens] that Faulkner so heartily condemns" (138).

Centering on the issue of language, Temple's creative powers are "evil" only in the sense that they have not been adequately symbolized to the community; she is "irresponsible" only to the degree that she has not yet communicated her conception of a modern technological society that makes room for love and honor as primary values. That this is her task is indicated by her constant questioning of the ambiguous platitudes of the men and women around her. Looking back, Temple comments to the Governor on "how anybody just seventeen and not even through freshman in college" had learned the erotic language which Temple had used in her amorous letters to Red (*Requiem* 130). The climax of Temple's struggle to find expression for her new role requires her to speak of Nancy's sacrifice as casting "the last gambit," that is "her own debased and worthless life" (*Requiem* 178-79). Significantly Temple speaks of holding together the child's "normal and natural home," another of the many indications that the modern Temple is overlaid against older and more conventional conceptions such as the ideal of a stable family "for the sake of the children."

Temple selects the word "gambit," which is the right word in that the suggestion of a sacrifice in chess introduces the idea of play, as if only the play of language in trope and metaphor will relieve the misleading seriousness of rhetoric. Later, Temple returns to the problem of language in challenging the slang of Nancy's assertion that she can "get low for Jesus" (234). Though she hesitates, Temple quickly embraces Nancy's language, recognizing that "that's the only language He arranged for you to learn" (235).

Temple defends Nancy's language just as she defends her life, suggesting a fundamental identity between herself and Nancy. As Temple indicates, their joint "doom" began at the same moment, "that morning eight years ago when I got on the train at the University" with Gowen Stevens. Like Nancy, Temple has chosen to reside in the Underworld of the modern city; she has created the world anew in the image of her desire and vision, yet in terms of her language, Temple is more precise and realistic. Nancy's speech sounds much like the sentimentalists at Miss Reba's establishment. Her religious views, derived from the theology of southern fundamentalism, are moralistic and conservative. Her homely expression of faith before her execution, while sincere, is certainly insufficient for Temple's needs.

The effect of Nancy's conventionality is to isolate Temple as the only representative of modernism, the survivor who will be required to continue living in the wasteland she has discovered. However, in no sense does Temple repudiate her experiment. What she affirms at the conclusion of *Requiem for a Nun* encompasses the moment eight years ago when she stepped off a train with the drunken Gowen Stevens. It encompasses and transforms her entire progress beyond the rural traditionalism from which she fled. Her own "gambit," grander even than that of Nancy Mannigoe, must be lived out in the daylight at the very center of the new culture. The reason why Temple did not attempt to flee from Popeye, following his lead even to the point of perjuring herself at the trial of Lee Goodwin, was her sense of the need to enter the ethical center of urban, industrial society and to play out her own self-sacrifice so that "good can come out of evil" (*Requiem* 179).

Temple's forgiveness of Nancy is also self-forgiveness, not only Temple's but Faulkner's blessing on the "evil" of modernity against which he had seemed to be arguing for so long. In finding ways to represent the aesthetic devastation of modernity, Temple (and Faulkner) is realizing ways to transform it. Temple explains that the night her son was killed by Nancy she learned "what" she must do: her difficulty is finding out "how." Temple seeks to make suffering explicable, just as Nancy had with her insistence on "belief." However, Temple's faith will not adopt the same shape as the belief in a literalist heaven expressed by Nancy. Temple has renounced none of her need to live in the present, to experience love fully, and to speak a language authentic to modern experience. These elements of modernist culture will help to determine the sort of faith at which she is able to arrive, if she is to arrive at any. Temple's difficulty at finding peace is coupled with her refusal to accept either death or exile, choices permitted other Faulknerian heroines such as Charlotte Rittenmeyer or Caddy Compson. With the last words of *Requiem for a Nun* Temple Drake continues as the central fictional presence, requiring the reader to absorb the full discomfort of her position. As with Flaubert's final, unsettling image of Emma Bovary before her death, the last glimpse of Temple Drake is sacrificial. Leaving the jail to join an unsympathetic husband and uncle, she is portrayed as a suffering and misunderstood originator whose transition to modernity is at times reckless, impulsive, and even destructive but never dishonest. She is the most uncompromising of Faulkner's women at the crossing of the ways, and her accomplishment is nothing short of a transformation of Faulkner's aesthetic in the presentation of women.

Chapter 5

Allen Tate and the Victorians

In his essay "A Reading of Keats" Allen Tate opens with an assessment of Victorian critics of Keats and specifically of Matthew Arnold, whose "almost perverse use of critical standards" resulted in his viewing Keats "quite simply as a 'sensuous' poet" who needed, according to Arnold, a greater sense of the poet's moral responsibility (*Essays* 263). According to Tate the dramatic-symbolic style of Keats had become inaccessible to the Victorian, whose difficulty with Keats suggested a more general cultural failing.

Tate's remarks on Arnold are typical of his lifelong concerns with the Victorians, who represent the product of historical "process" that has led to a dissociation of mind and feeling, an alienation of artist and community, an isolation of the present from a past of myth and tradition. It is striking then to read in the same passage that Tate's own "disabilities as a critic of Keats" are "not unlike Arnold's" (*Essays* 263). Indeed, the theme that pervades all of Tate's comments is "the lesson taught us by the Victorians"; it is that modernists now see what the Victorian could almost. Although he admitted the fact hesitantly, Allen Tate's poetry and criticism were strongly indebted to the very authors whom he frequently attacked. Understanding the continuity between Tate and his predecessors and tracing the reasons for Tate's need to dismiss their contributions may provide insight into modernist poetics and into Tate's role in the establishment of "Modernism" as a period of literary history which defines itself to a considerable extent in terms of its break with the Victorians.

Tate's effort to understand the modernist inheritance surfaces in the correspondence with Donald Davidson in the late 1920s and in essays that date from the same period. Because this was also a time of relative poetic inactivity, a period in which Tate had moved beyond his efforts at radical innovation, the mannered experimentation of his early poems of the Fugitive period, but had not found the mature style initiated with "Sonnets of the Blood," it is likely that Tate's scrutiny of the relation of Victorian and modernist poetics, valuable in its own right as perceptive criticism, was also fundamental to his own poetic evolution. For, in reality, Tate's criticisms of the Victorians are criticisms of the Victorian element in his own writing, and in the writing of his colleagues, Donald Davidson and John Crowe Ransom. Realizing that he could not simply dispel what he termed the "devastation" wrought by the Victorians but that he must work his way through it, Tate was compelled by some inner feature of his emotional life to salvage the past that had been lost. The compulsions of personal psychology and family history that Tate was perhaps exorcising in these efforts were cloaked by the severity of his devotion to the world of "letters," an insistence on the man of letters as responsible to the "perfection" of value in the work of art.

The announcement of having broken with the Victorians accompanied Tate's entrance into the world of letters. Tate wrote Davidson on 21 July 1922 of his "tendency to sympathize with almost anything revolutionary, sensible or not, and at the same time to derogate conservatism of all kinds" (Fain 20). After Davidson forwarded a satirical poem "Dryad," about which he felt considerable reservation, Tate welcomed his Vanderbilt colleague as a "Modern": "Whatever the limitations of us Moderns, we are certainly exploring, and giving voice to, a vast neglected field; others may do better in years to come--but so much for the originators" (Fain 13).

A similar spirit of investigating a "neglected field" underlies Tate's first volume *Mr. Pope and Other Poems* (1929) with such poems as "The Subway." However, even in this early sonnet, packed with much imagery of technological conquest of space, Modernism is balanced by a voice of moral commentary that seeks to humanize a world changed by mechanization, a dialogue not unlike the pioneering efforts of Thomas Carlyle and John Ruskin to come to understand industrialization. Later, in "Sonnets of the Blood, IX" Tate could use Carlyle's term "captains of industry." As Ferman Bishop points out, his "speaker rejects by his irony all the fatuous optimism of the nineteenth century associated with the term" (104). Nonetheless, the language of both poems is reminiscent of the "technological sublime" with which many Victorians described the industrial landscape. The poem is "modern" only in its intensification of reaction against technology, the hardening of moral stance conveyed in "iron forestries of hell" and "cold revery of an idiot" and in its techniques of discontinuity to suggest the extent of dislocation produced by technology.

At the time he wrote "The Subway" Tate's attitude toward the machine, which one might expect to be entirely uncompromising, relied on a distinctly Victorian ambivalent conception. As Herbert Sussman points out, since "the machine is both the unwearied iron servant and the sacrificial god to whom mankind has offered its soul," Victorian literary treatment often assumes the two oppositional modes of celebration and escape. Victorian writing "consistently opposes the organic to the mechanistic" as when Arnold opposes to machinery "the organic process of culture, in which the mind grows by fusing ethics and intellect" or Carlyle celebrates the machine in terms of the "technological sublime" that magnifies the sense of mystery and power, "arousing a fearful awe" (Sussman 7-30). "The Subway," a poem that Tate described to Davidson as depicting the "triumph of the machine," by its very attempt at striking a blow for the "new" achieves a highly mannered quality that reflects an assumption of Victorian concepts more than a reaction against them. This was the period when Tate was writing back to Davidson that "the great city of New York was his companion" (Fain 120-33). The example of Hart Crane revealed the direction he envisioned for his own writing, but the ambivalence toward the city that most readers detect in Allen Tate's early poetry derives from an effort not unlike Carlyle's to deal with mechanization by absorbing the machine into a transcendental philosophy. As Lewis Simpson shrewdly notes, "Carlyle's grand vision of men of letters as the priests of a restoration of an age of faith in the face of an age of science" had been adopted by Tate, who was always "writing a poem as an act symbolic of the mind's capacity for the perception of transcendence" (Fain ix-x).

Thus, while Tate spoke in terms of the "damage" done the moderns by the Victorians, his own literary apprenticeship grappled with identical problems and adopted similar stances. To define his own position as a modernist, Tate found it necessary to stress the devastation of the emotional and psychic life that had once been integrated around a central communal faith and that had, since breakdown of the classical-Christian worldview of medieval Europe, been sustained by the "man of letters." Though the process of devastation had been unfolding for centuries, the unique failing of the Victorian period, in Tate's view, was the general impoverishment of "letters," the realm of human endeavor that had continued to order the cultural life in the lapse of the authority of the church but that was now reduced to "faked" sentiment and spurious "culture."

In the place of a cultural tradition, Victorian science offered a purely evolutionary view of nature of the sort that Ruskin had opposed, the vision of nature as mechanism. Unable to attempt the kind of defense of organicism that Ruskin wrote in "The Relationship of Natural Science to Art" (1872), Tate surrendered nature to science, at least until the 1950s when Jacques Maritain's assumptions about the existence of natural order enter his writing. "Pastoral" represents very well the earlier view, which shows the natural world stripped of artifice and reduced to the level of scientific accidents. The even earlier poem "Cold Pastoral" has the poet reacting against "faithless" forces of nature whose bestiality may "fix you prone in their moon." Against the dangers of natural disorder the author seeks the authority of an aging persona similar to the "ancient" voices of some of Eliot's early poems. Tate writes in "Cold Pastoral" of touching the grass "with fearful cozenage." He identifies his frightened narrator as one who is a youth "zealous for old age." Less a solution to the problem of the scientific reduction of nature to the level of abstraction than a dramatization of the mind's confused opposition to it, "Cold Pastoral" marked the point in Tate's early poetry at which a hardening of the will as a mechanical response to Victorian science was still attractive enough to require the poet's refutation.

Like other modernists whose public rejection of Victorianism was based on a definition of their own aesthetic as transcending rhetoric, Tate intended a pure "transparent" poetry that promised a unified re-creation of experience without discourse. Though later critical statements imply that this was merely posited as an unattainable ideal, Tate's critical theory always relied on an almost mystical dynamic force that might mediate between artist and world. The manner in which meanings can explode from strained linkages of image in such early poems as "Bored to Choresis" or "Idyl" is Tate's homage to this dynamism, as is the more graceful interplay of intellect and intractable experience in "Seasons of the Soul" or "The Maimed Man" trilogy. The familiar initial stance of modernists involved a rejection of Victorian moralizing, an "antididacticism" that nonetheless created a myth of lost origins and thus a basis for authoritative knowledge. Paradoxically, each of the major modernist poets in turn developed increasingly didactic responses in the course of a longer career.

For the southern modernist, rhetoric would necessarily be understood in the light of the nineteenth-century South as well as English literary tradition. Yeats might distance the rhetorical style of the Victorians and yet preserve it in the guise of Crazy Jane's own dogmatizing, but the southern writer could hardly conceal a cultural identification with a moral idealism that paralleled the southern chivalric code of honor, a code that the southern writer might disclaim but that he still found necessary to a sense of common regional identity. Yeats would disguise and proceed to use the rhetorical mode; Tate found it necessary to disguise, use, and, simultaneously, proclaim the validity of rhetoric.

The similarity between Victorian rhetorical poetry and southern oratory must have been in Tate's mind, particularly after the completion of his study of southern history that culminated in his biography of its leading orator, Jefferson Davis. The danger and the attraction of rhetoric are still with him in the forties, for in "The Hovering Fly" he alludes to "a host of comforting saws that could easily turn this vascillating discourse into an oration" (*Essays* 113). A similarity between southern and Victorian culture underlies the attractiveness of rhetoric to each: the Victorians were, as Tate rarely tired of pointing out, seeking a rapprochement between art and science which would permit the "advancement" of modern culture based on the dissociation of mind and feeling, a positivist society in which the specialization of sensibility would eliminate contact with a unified organic culture; in place of the traditional, modern society asked its artists to create an abstract culture based on sentiment and social consciousness. It was Tate's remarkable insight, an insight that perhaps prevented him from completing his biography of Robert E. Lee, that the Old South's economy of chattel slavery, the plantation system devoted overwhelmingly to export trade, constituted a similar modern economy: its tendencies were hardly traditionalist, as Tate had once hoped to show, for it had been betrayed by its own obsessions with commerce and modernity. Southern writing had necessarily been rhetorical in mode, for it had been written in defense of an unacknowledged abstraction. The culture of the Old South, once proposed as the alternative to modernity, proved to be equally modern to the industrial economy of the Victorians. Paradoxically, it is the rhetorical quality of both Victorian poetry and southern oratory that Tate connects with the impetus in literary history toward Modernism. Though rhetoric must inevitably fail in its revelation of truth, rhetoric was profession, at least, of the writer's intentions toward authoritative knowledge. Speaking of his debt to the Victorian poet James Thomson, Tate states that Thomson's "inflated rhetoric and echolalia merely adumbrated the center of psychic and moral interest of later and better poets" (*Essays* 236).

Tate's critique of Victorian rhetoric centers on his objection to its having accommodated poetry to the demands of scientific rationalism. According to Tate's analysis, the Victorian poet relied on an abstract conception of "culture" that defended poetry from science by removing art from vital contact with life. The impasse for the early Tate, one that came to a head in the creative lull following the "Ode to the Confederate Dead," was the result of his conviction that the Victorians had failed to define the relationship between technique and subject. Since Tate believed that the modern poet cannot invent his theme, a point he emphasized in his 1924 review of Hart Crane, the modernists were left with only technique, an impulse to purify the language of the tribe without a significant theme: "We are an age of Minors, and our only raison d'etre is good technique, it seems to me" (Fain 111), Tate wrote Davidson. In later form, Tate's theory of the imagination, as set forth in his essay on Longinus, insisted on the interplay of technique and subject, art and life. He had once seen the modern age, largely consequent upon its inheritance from the nineteenth century, as a unique period in which artists were without a subject and must rely on technique alone; by the late forties, Tate began to speak of all periods of art as involving a condition of alienation of artist from subject. Tate quoted Longinus that "*we must learn from art the fact that some elements of style depend upon nature alone*" (*Essays* 479). Tate interpreted Longinus to mean that "the fusion of art and nature, of technique and subject, can never exceed the approximate; the margin of imperfection, of the unformed, is always there-- nature intractable to art, art unequal to nature" (*Essays* 480).

Tate's attitude toward poetic technique (indeed, his views in general on science, technology, positivism in the guise of social science or "culture") is the most paradoxical and troubling element of his relationship to the Victorians. His primary statement on the relation of science and literature, "Literature as Knowledge," begins with reference to Arnold's battle with the Philistines and the conclusion that "his program, culture added to science and perhaps correcting it, has been our program for nearly a century, and it has not worked" (*Essays* 72). The authorization of poetry by placing it on a "positive scientific base" from which it would take over the function of religion and successfully resist science was an inadequate solution: "the nicely co- operative enterprise of scientist and poet which the nineteenth century puts its faith in" has failed because the scientists were not interested in cooperation. The scientist was not "confined to the inertia of fact; his procedure was dynamic all along" (*Essays* 72-73). Arnold's defects of critical theory result in his belief that "the language of poetry is of secondary importance to the subject," for the "prose subject" of the poem is for Arnold on "the level of observation and description" and the language of poetry merely "conveys it and remains external to it" (*Essays* 76- 77). In sum, Arnold's poetics obscure the distinction between art and science, promote a static aesthetic, and center improperly on the subject rather than the language.

It would be difficult, I believe, to outline more clearly the weaknesses of Tate's own early poetry, or that of Davidson, or that of the Fugitives as a group. The rationalistic program of regional boosterism, the static rhetorical tone, the subject-dominance of the Fugitive verse borrowed a sense of authority in part from Arnold's influential criticism. If Tate's later poetry achieved passion, dynamism, and technical complexity, it was because he was engaged in a process of continual self-examination that exposed his affinities with the Victorians. The emphasis on technique in Tate's critical theory and in the New Criticism that he helped found is less an attack on Arnold's poetics than a parry or a self-disciplining act that assumes an aesthetic discomfort deriving from an acute knowledge of the Victorian legacy. Ultimately, Tate's critical evaluation of Arnold may be traced to what the modernist poet saw as the Victorian expansion of a romantic dissociation of sensibility.

The romantic dichotomy was related in Tate's mind to the issue of abstraction, the falsification of past and present experience through sentimentality or jargon. Turning from the concrete world of experience, the Victorian typically found self-authorization at the expense of personal involvement or "agency" in relation to the subject of the poem. Coleridge presented the modern dilemma between regarding poetry as metaphysic or psychology, intellect or feeling. Following the Romantics, the increasing loss of a sense of agency, a loss of connection between mind and objective world, in the works of the Victorians, particularly in Tennyson, signals the expansion of positivism, that as Tate defines it "is a world without minds to know the world" (*Reason* 59).

As Jerome H. Buckley notes in "The Persistence of Tennyson," Tennyson's poetry reflects a sense of the loss of agency except in rare moments of self-identity. As Jerome Buckley writes, "such intuitive experiences . . . were, as we know, familiar to Tennyson at intervals all his life, eclipses of the self but also guarantees of the self's meaning, and at least in their aftereffect, quickeners of the self's identity, agents (the psychologist would say) of 'the ego process' by which the individual maintains 'a subjective sense of invigorating sameness' and a coherence of past and present" (9). Even as he helped direct modern poetics away from the uncertain grasp of agency typified by Tennyson toward the intense agency of the modernist poem strongly marked by the poet's craftsmanship and rooted in the concrete image, Tate addresses tensions similar to those of Victorian poetics. A poetics that asserts the end of rhetoric and approaches an increasingly severe limitation of possibility of meaningful discourse except through the mediation of physical reality is the product of a lifetime of dialectic with problems that would have seemed familiar to many Victorian poets and critics.

Although Tate's short poems, brief moments of self-identity culled from a lifetime of doubt, are equivalent in some sense to Tennyson's intervals of self-awareness, Tate's frustrated attempts to complete a long epic poem may be traced to the same dilemma that faced his Victorian predecessors, and particularly to the dilemma of the poet-critic Arnold. Tate channeled much of his energy into the composition of a body of literary criticism which is among the most perceptive and extensive of our time, but to a considerable extent the criticism was written as a continuation of the poetry: advancing with the poetry, the criticism serves as a rhetorical assertion of modernist identity, defending an often insecure grasp of "agency" against the inertia of Victorian doubt. Through his criticism Tate was able to shore up the defenses of modernist identity to an extent only partially achieved in his poetry. Typically, the relationships of poet, poem, and world were analyzed with the Victorian example in mind. Despite his frequent repudiation of all things Victorian, Tate's project of transforming modern poetics is bound up with his fascination with those metaphysical dilemmas that are dramatized in Victorian poetry: the dissociation of intellect and emotion, the elimination of poem from world, the loss of a sense of poetic agency.

Perhaps as a result of his ambivalence toward the South, Tate paid close attention to the relation of poetry and history, and to the idea of a possible "recovery" of the past through the imagination. Indeed, the crux of Tate's complaints concerning the Victorian aesthetic, and the point that most clearly connects his own poetry with theirs, is the treatment of the past and the debasement of the traditional in modern culture. Tate traces the submission of the writer to a crisis of modern history that involves the reduction of historical actuality to an abstraction. The ambivalent example of Robert Browning, a poet whose self-exhausting discourse might be viewed either as an attempt to evoke historical actuality or an effort to evade it through language, did not escape Tate's notice. In an essay on Thomas Hardy, Tate claims that Browning did not hold with Hardy's "single-mindedness" to the "mechanistic theories of his time" (*Essays* 339). Elsewhere, in "A Note on Elizabethan Satire" Tate speaks of "resistance of the language to full expression, the strain between images and rhythm" that gives "to English lyrical verse its true genius," an effect that appears in Wyatt, Milton, Dryden, and surprisingly in Browning (*Essays* 258-59). Out of this tradition of poetry emerges the modern symbolist movement of which Tate is a late example, a tradition continued, as Bruce Michelson implies, in the confessional poetry of Robert Lowell (39).

What Tate believed to be the solipsism implicit in the Victorian attitude toward history is one subject of the "Ode to the Confederate Dead." The "lone man by the gate" recalling past heroism is also the modern poetic sensibility, reenacting the "failure of the human personality to function objectively in nature and society" (*Reason* 136). The meditation in Tate's "Ode" is essentially a Victorian legacy: the acceptance of a fragmentary cosmos in which an impasse between desire and action reduces the personality to an indecisive perceiver separated from its world (the Prufrock figure who steps into Eliot's early poetry out of Tennyson's narrators) or the reduction to a purely naturalistic level of experience. The modern at the gate elegizes the end point of western civilization ("The cold pool left by the mounting flood/Of muted Zeno and Parmenides"), a posture that Tate noted in Oswald Spengler's influential contemporary work, *The Decline of the West* ("Fundamentalism" 532-34). The objective authority of history, a requirement for the "chivalry" that the screech-owl celebrates in "tight/Invisible lyric," is smothered like a "mummy" by consciousness of the self's participation in historical process. In the ironic questioning ("What shall we say who have knowledge/Carried to the heart?") one suspects a doubling of meaning by which both the sentimental and the rationalistic level of Victorian discourse are suggested. The ambivalence of the lines conveys both the trivialization of knowledge (knowledge "carried to the heart" in terms of sentiment) and the rationalization of emotion, the heart displaced by specialized knowledge that denotes only function. The solipsism of Victorian writing was connected with what Tate considered a falsification of history through nostalgia and poetic technique that separated the poet-as-agent from his creation. Yet it is at just such moments when he is most perceptive, as in his critique of Tennyson's historicism, that he is also most selective and prone to distortion of his own relationship to the Victorians.

So convincing is Tate's rhetoric that we may at times fail to see it as the argument of a modernist constructing his own period of literary history. Tate's arguments for the shape that Modernism ought to assume may be traced in large measure to his early reaction against Victorian abstraction and sentimentality. On closer examination, an underlying continuity appears in the similarity with which Tate labored against the problems of historical and personal abstraction. Insistence on historical accuracy and emphasis on the contemporary culture is tied to Tate's belief that the power of the artist-as-creator is limited in relation to the cosmos that includes him. The dilemma for the modern poet was how to reintegrate human civilization around a new mythology that avoided a nostalgic return to a distant past (the Gothicism of the late Victorians) while skirting the self-idolatry that voicing of the new mythology implied. Tate's strategy involved a reversal of the Victorian effacement of agency: never permitting his reader to lose sight of the limited human agent who creates poetry only in the restricted sense of one whose creations bear the gashes of self-criticism and failure, Tate's poems balance an insistence on agency against a weighty program of spiritual and aesthetic transformation.

The abstraction of experience that Tate fears, and that his intense short poems are continually dispelling, is represented in "Last Days of Alice," one of Tate's finest original poems on a Victorian theme. In her old age, Alice's "wonderland" has become self-deceptive and narcissistic, with "Alice grown lazy, mammoth but not fat." As in Ransom's beautifully compassionate poems about the loss of feminine beauty, the chief feature of the naturalistic world with which Alice's mind is not able to deal is time. As he captures the world of Alice's imagination, it is essentially a grotesquely static place where all life and nature are "forever," and where Alice grows fat without true consciousness "in the deep suspension of the looking-glass"(*Poems* 38).

Through the image of the frozen "grass," a favorite symbol for Tate of the natural world at its most particular and transient and thus most threatening to human mortality, the poem expresses the danger of the abstracting response to the condition of mortality. As with all who are unable to symbolize the fear of death through the creative imagination, Alice has created an illusory "double." The "All-Alice" has replaced the "world's entity," the self has replaced the world, and thus denied the existence of time and history. The historical "method" that replaces history is connected in the poem with science and the scientific view of time, a world-absorbed history filtered through and controlled by the human mind but comprising only arbitrary experience riven from integral design. Alice has broken with her "earthly twain," the limited self existing in the world, at the very moment when she plunged through the looking-glass.

"Last Days of Alice" marks a point at which Tate had begun to work through some of the more superficial problems of the Victorian and modernist relation. As Radcliffe Squires points out, the poem identifies the psyche of aging Alice with narcissism and abstraction, and it suggests that Alice's ignorance of evil is supported by her ego and faith in natural science (113). Alice exemplified the failure of Victorian culture to demand personal responsibility for the material basis for life, a crucial element in Tate's view for human society. Tate's political views harken back to the pre-modern position of Edmund Burke, who, as Raymond Williams shows, rejected the growing clamor for the "idea of the State as the necessary agent of human perfection" and insisted on an organic society with emphasis on "interrelation and continuity of human activities." The terms in which Williams categorizes Burke remind one of Tate's campaign for Agrarianism: insistence on the particularity of culture as the basis of a nation, "the peculiar circumstances, occasions, tempers, dispositions, and moral, civil, and social habitudes of the people, which disclose themselves only in a long space of time." What Tate found menacing in much Victorian social philosophy was typified by Arnold's opposition of Philistines and "aliens," those leaders of education and culture who would be led by humane and not by class spirit. Because of his lapse of faith in a transcendent order, "culture" slips to the level of abstraction, for Arnold had "admitted reason as the critic and destroyer of institutions, and so could not rest on the traditional society which nourished Burke" (Williams 128).

If Tate seemed always to be critical of the Victorians, it was because he sensed the need to distance himself from them. The history of Tate's struggle to translate Apollodorus's *Pervigilium Veneris*, an effort that lasted from 1917 until 1943, is representative of a lifelong effort to come to terms with Victorian poetics. Encountering the poem in Pater's *Marius the Epicurean*, Tate's early reading was thwarted by his being too close in his very revolt against the Victorians "to read properly any poem about pagan love" reminiscent of the love poems he recalled from Swinburne (*Poems* 145). Returning to the work in 1930, Tate failed to work out a translation of the refrain that avoided the cadence, as he said, "of Tennyson's *Locksley Hall*" (*Poems* 145). The process of aesthetic development and understanding that Tate sketches is one of revolt against the Victorian poetic, followed by a period in which he struggled to find an independent sensibility, succeeded in turn by a confident assumption of his own aesthetic that allowed an acknowledgement of the Victorian legacy. It is a journey which in the end seems necessary to the modernist poet's achievement of an independent poetic.

Chapter 6

Allen Tate's Treatment of Mechanization

"Our time cleaves to no racial myth, its myth is the apotheosis of machinery," wrote the young Allen Tate, excited by his friend Hart Crane's effort to forge a modern literary myth from the fragmented images of contemporary America. In a review of *The Bridge* in which he assessed the impact of mechanization on modern life and discussed strategies for aesthetic responses, Tate praised Crane's enormous ambition but noted the absence of "an objective pattern of ideas elaborate enough to carry it through an epic of heroic work." His friend Crane possesses unequaled talent which produces "magnificent short flights" and "beautiful inventions," but his structural idea "is not sufficiently objective and articulate in itself." Unlike the successful epic of Dante whose "invention" combines discipline and "groundwork," Crane fails at the longer poem because of his "unphilosophical belief that the poet, unaided and isolated from the people, can create a myth" ("A Distinguished Poet" 582-83).

From this early review one learns perhaps more about Tate than Crane. Tate shared the ambition of composing an epic that would in its own way be as contemporary as *The Bridge* (in fact, he attempted to work on an epic poem during his Guggenheim stay in France in 1930). Much is said in Tate's review about the necessity of an "objective" basis for artistic creation, a problem that would become the central dilemma of his attempt to confront the modern inheritance of nineteenth-century aesthetics. If it were true that "no one man ever put myth into history," as Tate had insisted in his review of Crane, how could the modern poet, largely isolated from his audience and from a true community of other authors, hope to forge an aesthetic theory which would permit a reintegration of the epic sensibility? If poetry required a vital culture of myth and tradition, were not all his efforts doomed to the level of "personal" inventions resulting in the sort of obscurity or sentimentality that Tate identified in Crane's heroic efforts?

The dilemma seemed all the more acute to Tate as a young southern poet outside the mainstream of American letters, as he must have felt himself to be, coming of age in Winchester, Kentucky, and in Nashville, during the first decades of the century. If so, Tate and other young southern writers found support for a time in their Fugitive association at Vanderbilt University. Donald Davidson, whose correspondence with Tate covered a period of some fifty years, was possessed of the sanguine belief that the poet might recall the mythic basis for epic from his regional history, an approach that Tate must have felt was another heroic but doomed effort to "put myth into history." Davidson's *The Tall Men* confronts the same dilemma as had emerged in Tate's reflections on Crane. Davidson's poet-figure, pondering the lost arcadia of his dead father, describes the futurist city of steel and glass in which he lives. The "Prologue: The Long Street" celebrates the legendary events of early settlement and the Civil War in contrast with the modern "pig's conception of the state," just as Davidson's letters to Tate portray modernity as "the enemy," a force opposed to the traditional society of community and history.

Looking back over his early career, Davidson would define Agrarianism as "the cause of civilized society, as we have known it in the Western World, against the new barbarism of science and technology controlled and directed by the modern power state" (*Southern Writer* 45). Davidson's oppositional perspective produced such unsubtle satires as "Conversations in a Bedroom," in which the modern Ego finds life unsatisfying and sees a filmed procession of pseudo-prophets: A Traveler, The Mystic, Three Expatriates, Satyr in a Tuxedo, Bobbed-Hair Bacchante, and An Intellectual. Another opposition of modernity and tradition, "The Breaking Mould," presents three figures (pagan, Methodist, and scientist) which need to be reconciled by an Evangelist with a new "scroll." Davidson writes: "I see the God/Who will not tame the manliness of man" (*Poems* 170).

The productive tension which might have arisen from Davidson's recognition of the competing claims of modern life and traditional society was suppressed in his poetry, in which clear-cut "solutions," the imposition of legendry or religious moralizing as aesthetic authority, tamed the authentic psychological conflicts that surface uncensored in his fine letters to Tate, Andrew Lytle, and others. If Davidson's denial of a rupturing within the poet was one "solution" to the dilemma facing the Fugitives, John Crowe Ransom offered his own refutation, a logical balancing that preserved the tensions but also repressed the emotional threat of change. The formal quality of diction and metrics which Ransom uses to treat his one important theme, the "frailty of women's beauty," (Stewart 239), freezes the inevitable human failure to attain the moral ideal within a perfected formalism. In this respect Ransom's concept of poetry resembles a theory of religion and myth that ritualizes the limitation of human power in relation to the unlimited will of a transcendent being. "Blue Girls" is at the same time compassionate and impersonal as Ransom states, "And I will cry with my loud lips and publish/Beauty which all our power shall never establish." The self-absorption of the blue girls in their own beauty is appropriately published by the ironic "loud lips," a clumsiness of style that matches the unperspicacious adolescence of the girls. Nonetheless, the moving elegiac quality of the poem as a whole does record the girls' beauty and the tragedy of its inevitable loss. In such well-known poems as "Dead Boy," "Bells for John Whiteside's Daughter," and "Here Lies a Lady," the discrepancy between subject and treatment dramatizes the "inevitable" disappointment of human desire.

Only in a few poems does Ransom directly address the subject of mechanization, yet the ironic play of wit in such important works as

"Man Without a Sense of Direction," "Necrological," and "Persistent Explorer" points toward the poet's discomfort with modernization. Even poems that do not speak directly to the issue of change seem to project underlying concerns with the disparity between traditional conceptions of human nature and the contemporary realities. Ransom's best poems establish a momentary identity between speaker and object, an intimacy that by its conspicuous presence exaggerates the surrounding alienation of feeling in the poem. As in "Here Lies a Lady," where Ransom's sensibility resists the modernist tendency to displace the representation of grief with sexuality, a displacement of romantic love with realism which seemed to Ransom to threaten a fundamental rapport between man and his environment, the poem's "defense" of traditionalism protests too much. Ransom's insistence on a formality of diction and stanza simply discloses a poetry which, as Tate came to feel, abdicated the "real" world of contemporary affairs to scientific rationalism. The problem with Ransom's formalism, from Tate's perspective, was not that Ransom was too "traditional"; rather, it was that Ransom credited too highly the power of science and technology and so refused to confront them. In looking back, it may have come as little surprise to Tate that Ransom's insistence on traditionalism was softened in *The New Criticism* (1941) and in his later essays on the relationship of art and science.

The well-reasoned "refutation" of mechanistic philosophy worked out in Ransom's early prose, especially in *God Without Thunder* (1930), and the example of his highly successful poems, which had earned him a reputation abroad as a leading American poet, served Tate in many ways. Nonetheless, when Ransom all but abandoned writing poetry and at the same time repudiated Agrarianism in the late Thirties, Tate had only begun to enter his most productive phase. Tate shared Ransom's concept of nature as "quality" or, in Tate's phrase, "a conglomerate of violence and decay that stands for the psychic life of modern man" (quoted in Stewart 312). For both writers, only escape from the self and from nature into a higher order of experience would bring freedom. Following Ransom's lead,

Tate's early essay "Humanism and Naturalism" attacked science for resorting to abstract systems ("Quantity") as a means of dealing with the anarchic thrust of nature ("Quality"). Not only the incursion of science but also the increasing trust in a world political order disturbed Tate. "The New Provincialism" (1945) arrived at conclusions about totalitarianism that had been implicit in his earliest writing. Tate wrote that "provincialism is that state of mind in which regional men lose their origins in the past and its continuity into the present and begin every day as if there has been no yesterday."

Given the similarity of their analysis of the impact of modernization on art and society, what accounts for the different aesthetic approaches of Ransom and Tate? The essential difference, I believe, lies in the fact that unlike Ransom, who could seem to distance the threat of modernity in the aesthetic formalism of the poem (regardless of whether this "distancing" revealed an equal if not greater discomfort), Tate was compelled to confront modernity more directly and personally, in relation to his own experiences, recognizing the mechanistic principles operating within his own region, history, and psyche.

That Tate was dealing with contemporary issues is apparent even in his early "historical" writing. His historical imagination is peculiarly fascinated with seeing history as present; no "historical" event can interest Tate unless it has been grasped as a part of his own psychological experience. Thus, his Civil War biographies of Stonewall Jackson, Jefferson Davis, and Robert E. Lee are not parochial defenses of the Lost Cause but dramatic projections of Tate's inner conflicts over his art and his role as a "modern." By the time he composed "Remarks on the Southern Religion" (later reprinted as "Religion and the Old South") for the Agrarian collection of 1930, *I'll Take My Stand*, Tate had already arrived at the conclusion that the Old South's attempt to evolve a humane community on the European model had failed because its religious life "was not enough organized with a right mythology" (*Collected Essays* 320).

"The South would not have been defeated," Tate flatly asserted, "had she possessed a sufficient faith in her own kind of God" (*Collected Essays* 321). As late as 1930 Tate might still hope that by political organization the South might yet overcome the "setback of the war" and re-establish a traditional society, yet research in connection with his southern biographies and his novel *The Fathers* increasingly undermined this conviction. Jefferson Davis represented an "inability to bring intellect and emotion together," a "self-conquered" man, a master of rhetoric committed to abstract principles rather than the emotional defense of what was good in the South (Squires 97). In Lee's career Tate perceived something worse, a Virginian born "perfect" and "self-contained," capable of inexhaustible ambition but not of devotion to an objective principle, a leader possessed of an ambition which no worldly reward would satisfy: [Lee's personality] "feeds upon its own perfection and drops its participation in affairs the moment this inner integrity is threatened" (Squires 97). The intellectual perfection that isolated Lee from the human community seemed analogous to Crane's failure, for both had failed to submit the ego to nature. Both conceived of invention in terms of a self-reflexive romanticism. With this aesthetic Lee and Crane were examples of men who were bound to reject the richness of both past and present. Both lacked a truly historical imagination because they had failed to salvage history from process.

"Remarks on the Southern Religion" pointed the direction for further discussion of modernization. As the most impassioned defender of Agrarianism, even after the defection of Ransom and Warren, "Tate had needed the South, as he seemed to need many things, as a way of escaping from the burden of a limited self into a homogenous society, a world that might satisfy his thirst for an authoritative context of ideas" (O'Brien 160). Paradoxically, Tate's thinking on Agrarianism and southern history only brought him to greater uncertainty concerning the authority which he sought. In the wake of his defense of the Agrarian South, Tate arrived at a position of radical uncertainty. I am not certain that O'Brien's description of Tate's conversion to Catholicism ("In the long run, he chose a more conventional path toward ideological authority" 160) connotes the condition of personal devastation from which Tate embraced Catholicism, nor the uncertainties that marked his psychology after his conversion. As his interest in Agrarianism as a socio-political solution waned, Tate moved against what for him had always been the central threat of modernity: the disorder of the emotional and aesthetic life resulting from abstraction.

The imagery of the modern city proved a convenient vehicle for the expression of this disorder. Already, *Mr. Pope and Other Poems* (1928) projected imagery similar to Crane's urban setting but with considerably more ambivalence. The tone of Baudelairean decadence is unmistakable in "The Subway," the well-known poem which concludes the book's initial section on "Space." As Louis D. Rubin stresses, "What Tate wishes to show about the subway is its self-destructive, Satanic ugliness, its debasement of dignity and beauty for the sake of efficiency. But he realizes that the attitudes that created it include those of misdirected love, warped aesthetic craving, mistaken pride; it is hurtling toward hell not merely mechanistically but *religiously*, and in so doing it has its own beauty and grandeur" (121).

The crux of Tate's attitude toward mechanization is his analysis of the human relationship to the natural world. Mechanization is a misdirected flight from the primitive condition of nature, the savage, unimproved pastoral world in which human life is reduced to insignificance in the face of the larger processes of organic change. According to this view, mechanization is not the dehumanizing, repressive enslavement which, as we have seen, romantic and Victorian commentators often suggested, but an entirely understandable if unsympathetic strategy for avoiding the crushing pressure of primitive nature. Tate shows that mechanization arose from the impulse to establish human civilization against the chaos and flux of the primitive world, a motive that would have been particularly resonant for a southern writer of Tate's generation who could recall the fairly recent periods of the Civil War and Reconstruction in which the South's economy and civic life had been severely disrupted. The level of primitive nature was historically too familiar to the southerner of Tate's generation to permit any sort of idealizing. Clearly, at least in so far as it was experienced by southern modernists, the pastoral world seemed to harbor a menacing, irrational, pitiless movement toward dissolution.

Tate had not yet clearly formulated his ideas on the mythic function of the religious imagination which "checks the abstracting tendency of the intellect in the presence of nature" (*Reactionary Essays* 142). Thus, "Ode to the Confederate Dead" represents an intermediate stage in Tate's understanding of modernization. From the initial irony of the title, the "ode" which Tate inserted for the original "Elegy" for a poem which is not a public celebration but a private meditation, the entire piece adopts a strategy of self-critical discourse similar to that which Tate must have felt in asserting his public role as "man of letters" during the 1920s. The poem examines and rejects two familiar elements of the modern ethos, naturalism and solipsism. Of naturalism the poet asks: "Shall we. . . set up the grave/In the house?" On the other hand, the crab and jaguar are symbols of the locked-in ego of the modern intellectual severed from the world (Squires 77). Like T. S. Eliot's "Prufrock" and Wallace Stevens' "Sunday Morning," the "Ode" is "a meditation on the relationship between subjective and objective worlds" (Squires 81). Following a desperate but frustrated attempt to find a point of connection with the ritual order which the headstones embody, the poet finds that the heroic order rising out of "the immoderate past" cannot serve his needs. The refrain which Tate added to the poem suggests a fragmentary consciousness, like leaves separated from life, randomly blown by a wind of abstract intellect.

The "Ode" reveals Tate's admiration of Eliot in its many echoes of *The Waste Land* and "The Love Song of J. Alfred Prufrock." More specifically, Eliot influenced the language with which Tate chose to address the issue of modernization. The theory of the dissociation of sensibility dominates one of Tate's early essays published in *Outlook* (15 August 1928) in which Tate saw in Emily Dickinson a fusion of intellect and sensibility, a poetry that incorporates the individual talent within the Puritan tradition. However, seeing the issue of mechanization in terms of Eliot's theory of dissociation was ultimately of little use to Tate, for there is a fundamental difference of outlook underlying Tate's and Eliot's views of modernity. Tate's attraction to a perfect moral order which can never be attained by human effort conflicts with Eliot's apparent faith in the institutions of the church and in a conservative political order aided by the "orthodox" poet as the means of reaching some sort of "victory" over the mechanical element in modern existence, an oppositional aesthetic not fundamentally unlike Davidson's in many respects. The emphasis on failure in Tate's work and the severely self-critical tone of his best poems contrast with the greater sense of resolution achieved in Eliot's work, which seems tied to the modernist belief in the mind's ability to reconstruct tradition and myth. Tate's broken, abrupt, ironic endings mirror his conviction that modern consciousness has severed its link with the past of myth and that poetry lacks the power to summon the authorizing agency of history. Tate's aesthetic differs with the modernist faith in the individual poet's role as creator and myth-maker; in Tate's more humble and skeptical assessment, the poet performed the limited function of embodying his contemporary culture and perhaps of staving off the fragmentation. In this respect Tate's aesthetic theory is tied to his religious belief: the artist is severely limited in relation to the transcendent order which includes him. The dilemma for the religious poet was how to reintegrate human civilization around a new mythology, since any return to the past involved the falsification of historicism or nostalgia, while at the same time avoiding the self-idolatry implied in the role of poet-as-creator.

Another way of explaining the distinction between Tate and Eliot is to suggest that Tate held a more "private" vision. As Radcliffe Squires writes: for Tate "the heroic, the saintly act is a subjective, even a hidden, act of such private intensity that its public implementation is only an inevitable step, not a great step. . . Eliot's poetry has no *private* morality. His figures are either public saints or paralyzed puppets" ("Will and Vision" 560). From Tate's perspective Eliot failed precisely when he achieved his fullest *public* success, for his creation of a unified and ordered "still point" seemed dependent on the prideful creativity of the artist, an attempt of the sort of "perfection" which at first attracted Tate to, then repelled him from, Robert E. Lee.

The tendency for modern thinking to become at once mechanical and solipsistic which had been represented in the "Ode to the Confederate Dead" received more detailed analysis in the essays which Tate collected in *Reason in Madness* and *The Forlorn Demon*. Beginning in the late thirties, Tate's perspective, which could never have been termed hopeful, became direly pessimistic. He began to trace the rise of Positivism, a historical development associated with the suppression of freedom in the United States during the Second World War, an encroachment aided by the rise of social science and more threatening than fascism because disguised under the terms "democracy" and "liberalism." The effects of this "pseudo-democratic intellectual tradition" (*Reason* 7) were well advanced in the area of aesthetics and were beginning to corrupt the sensibility of the writers on whom the vitality of the language, and thus of society, depended.

Tate was profoundly affected by the display of American power during the Second World War, though unlike William Faulkner, who seemed to shift his aesthetic in significant ways to accommodate a patriotic embrace of American military force, Tate remained ambivalent toward the mobilization of industrial production which the war necessitated. In three important poems ("Jubilo," "More Sonnets at Christmas," and "Ode to Our Young Pro-consuls of the Air") the war effort is assailed as a resort to mechanized barbarism. The final stanzas of the "Ode" connect the pre-human with the technological stages of history: translated into Agrarian terms, the airplane, piloted with "cunning sense" through its "dreamless" sleep, lacks a traditional basis of life from which to draw mythic representation. The young pilots are only "like men," not wholly human, and their faith is with "imperial eye/I." The technological prowess of the West is exterminating the mythic sensibility of the past symbolized by "the Lama, late survival of old pain."

Such an uncompromising response to the ethical questions raised by mechanized warfare was possible because Tate viewed mechanized war from the perspective of a former Agrarian, and also because he transposed some of his own ambivalent identity as a southerner and late Modernist to his criticism of a narrowly patriotic literature. The war harnessed the sort of efficient industrial system that the Agrarians had feared, and the lapse of authentic poetry into a serviceable rhetoric was unmistakable in the work of "engaged" poets such as Archibald MacLeish.

Although the reasons behind Tate's response to the war may be clear enough, the position for these poems within the canon of his poetry is problematic, for they arrive at "solutions," or at least conclusions, which seem uncharacteristically simple. The artistic tension underlying the "Ode to the Confederate Dead" has hardened into polemic, and the dynamic metaphors have been reduced to emblems. Tate summons the "unreal" quality of the war in "More Sonnets at Christmas," in which "The American people fully armed. . ./Battle the world of which they're not at all." The "little boys go into violent slumber" deceived by the State's rhetoric, dying for God and country: "Their fear/ Is of an enemy in remote oceans/ Unstalked by Christ." The imagery of "Jubilo" includes the airplane, the fox-hole, and the accountant, concluding with the nightmarish transfusion of salt serum into the patient whose blood has been drained.

Upon closer examination, the war poems may be seen in their confident assumption of a posture of loss as enabling acts of self-authorization leading to the powerful later poems, in which the technical features of the war poems, a precision of image and statement, formal complexity within structured stanza, attention to the doubling of meanings and the exact suggestion of language, also advance beyond the early poetry and lead to the accomplishment of such works as "The Maimed Man" trilogy.

The association of Yeats with war in "Winter Mask" is striking, for war is the devastation at which historical process has arrived from Yeats' aesthetic in which the device of the "mask" assumes a fragmented relation between language and the world. Tate's poem is about technological warfare and the relationship of art and personal conviction: in short, the dialectic between art and history through which the modern poet achieves the sense of self-authorization. The Dantean scenes in "Winter Mask" prefigure "The Symbolic Imagination," the important post-war essay which addresses this very problem of poetic agency, the poet's sense of authority to create in the face of an external world which seems mechanical and fragmented by inauthentic experience. In this essay Tate is still working with the problem that haunted him since his reading of Crane: the difficulty of significant creation in a world in which the poetic temperament felt itself to be separated from everyday experience. In other terms, Tate was addressing the loss of audience for high culture, the decline of mass taste in an age of popular entertainment, yet he could not take refuge in elitism or private visions. He felt it necessary to find a basis for art in general experience.

"To bring together various meanings at a single moment of action is to exercise what I shall speak of here as the symbolic imagination," Tate wrote, "but the line of action must be unmistakable, we must never be in doubt about what is happening" (*Essays* 427). This new aesthetic theory bears an important relation to Tate's war experience , for the "compelling line of action" for the first time replaces the fragmentation and sense of isolation in the poetic persona which characterizes the earlier poetry. The belief that artistic truth is literally mirrored in the physical body of things is a belief based on the existence of a "vast anagogical structure" in the world. In terms that seem remarkably contemporary, he analyses the Illuminative Way in terms of "the 'distance' between us and what we see which is always the distance between a concept and its object, between the human situation in which the concept arises and the realization of its full meaning" (*Essays* 433). Anticipating the distinction between "knowing" and "understanding" in contemporary aesthetic theory, Tate had spoken of representation in terms of the representational situation rather than the fixed object, sign, or reference.

The promotion of New Criticism involved much more than rejection of the "genteel tradition" of historical criticism which Tate described in "Miss Emily and the Bibliographers," for in his mind the New Criticism was an outgrowth of his long struggle against the swelling tide of positivist science. By entering into a relationship with the complexities of language in the literary work, the critic celebrated the dynamic and vital qualities of literature while at the same time projecting his or her own incompleteness or inadequacy. If Tate had once declared that modern writers were merely technicians, because the loss of larger community centered on myth had undermined significant themes, he believed very much the opposite and continued to search for wholeness and significance throughout his career. The New Criticism assumed to some extent the existence of a unified community of cultured readers who would approach the literary work if not as a repository of truth, at least as a transforming experience. In the end, however, the direction that New Criticism took with its mechanical insistence on explication did not fairly represent Tate's mature view.

The New Criticism was shaped in part by Tate's understanding of mechanization. His analysis of aesthetics had begun with the assumption of nature as a process of dissolution antithetical to human civilization. In the face of this disorder, human society had produced abstract systems for the control of nature: science, mechanized industry, and capitalist economics were the components of a belief in secular progress as a bulwark against the entropy of nature. The rise of empirical science resulted in an equally mechanical reaction in the abstracting sensibility of Romanticism, which, threatened by the positivist claims of science, "invented" poetic imagination as a realm separate from the empirical world. The form of romantic imagination which abandons the real world to scientific explanation was termed "angelism," an abstracting flight from common reality that one found in the works of Poe, Emerson, Whitman, Crane, and Stevens in America, and in the Symbolist movement in France. Clearly, Tate saw his own writing as imperilled by the same romanticism, so he anchored his imaginative vision in the natural world without reducing it to naturalism. As outlined in "The Symbolic Imagination" the transcendent order was mirrored through the natural world; the essay presented a dramatic model for a perception of transcendence mirrored through the "common things" of the actual world.

Tate understood that New Criticism, while it avoided the "substitution of method" in historical criticism, could potentially become even more mechanical. Unlike Tate, who had recognized very early the dangers of positing a separate realm for the literary imagination, others in the same critical group appeared to assert an order of truth for the imagination distinct from empirical reality, an order of truth carried by the art work and superior to everyday knowledge. From Tate's perspective, these critics were still operating within the Coleridgean scheme which "preserved" literature from science by abandoning reality. In addition, the methodology of the New Criticism wrongly implied that the literary work possessed truth that was inherent in the work, a fact which reduced the dynamic process of reading to a mechanical task, no matter how complex. This procedure was very far from Tate's own practice of criticism, in which the reader staked everything in a dialogue with a literary work which was itself the projection of the author's distance from authority and from a reified idead of the "truth."

In his poetry as in his criticism, Tate is among the most sensitive of modern writers to the psychological damage of mechanistic or authoritarian approaches. The horror conveyed in "Seasons of the Soul," Section III (Winter), derives from the poet's understanding of the difficulty of love's existence in the face of the ego's drive toward security and completion. The poem begins with his plea to the goddess Venus to return to the sea and to leave the burnt earth, the modern wasteland for which the sacrificed god above "No longer bears for us/The living wound of love." The transformation of the goddess' vital love based on risk and mutability into a deadening modern love with its illusion of permanence is described in a Dantean stanza which suggests Paulo and Francesca. Following stanzas compare the failure of love to lower circles, in which purely animalistic passion is described.

The section on winter ends with an allusion to Dante's Wood of the

Suicides. In images that antedate "The Maimed Man" trilogy, the poet describes a headless oak: drowned, rigid, leafless. The oak recalls the rigid formalism of Tate's own early modernist efforts, a flight from the natural world toward mechanism that the poet now views as suicide. The poet feels the suicides' blood drip on his head and knows himself as "their brother." Like the suicides in the Inferno, Tate feels that he is wounded, and like the suicides he has refused to "bear the wound of love," that is, to continue living with the painful burden of human connections and loves.

The major accomplishment of Tate's later poetry is the trilogy consisting of "The Maimed Man," "The Swimmers," and "The Buried Lake." This trilogy of poems is, in fact, a rehearsal of the poet's development of an aesthetic as a response to the sense of contemporary mechanism. In the first poem the nightmare image of a headless man appears, a double of the poet who "thought that he could never do me harm." The head has been replaced by "the rusty play/Of light," an enlightenment that is connected with abstraction, an intellectual life-in-death. The poet fails to do what he "ought," to put the body into a "fast" grave. Honor forbids him from being known as the slave of his mortality, for the "manners" of modernity preclude the disclosure of the "secret" which human limitation and mortality comprise. The "scarecrow" which modern man is remains hidden to the poem until he sees in his mirror that he is also a "maimed man," entombed by the "willed" poetics that he had adopted as a strategy to ward off the frightening presence of his own mortality. A transition toward acceptance of mortality accompanies the recollection of the natural sensuous experience of childhood. The child's submission of self to nature had been repressed by the proud adolescent; the aging poet recovers the child's knowledge and sees what the child could not, the face of his dead mother "whose subtle down" he had not perceived while alive.

Set during Tate's childhood in Kentucky, "The Swimmers" recalls a child's observations of a lynching, an act which Tate connects with the special dangers of modernity as it attempts to deal with mortality through abstraction. The poem's title refers to the narrator, his childhood friends, the town, and the lynched Negro, who represents Christ: all are swimmers struggling to remain mortal and unharmed, but all seek the water as refreshment and life. Through the contrapuntal images of water/dryness, youth/age, and dream/waking, the poem reaches its understanding of the fundamental human attraction to both life and death, yet the poet never relinquishes his idealism: his intention is to return to and perhaps surpass the condition of love that he knew in early childhood. This form of renewal will occur only after the poet has represented the contemporary situation concretely, in other words, only after modernity has entered the dialectic of the poem. Drawing close to his "edge of darkness," that is, his mortality, the poet asks the Lady to "light up my edge of fear."

Even from childhood his intelligence has falsified the light which the Lady embodies, a denial of the "buried lake" of vitality which is parallelled by contemporary culture's reliance on abstract intellect. As an "ageing child" the poet has fled "like a squirrel to a hollow bole," the dark emptiness of intellect or self which denies the "leafy" particularity of the natural world. He stumbles on a shore "where time, unfaced, was dark," and his desolation climaxes in an inferno-like room in which he plays the "Devil's Trill" on violin but is halted by a dancing girl with a "soft surd," the posing of a problem which cannot be answered. Facing the paradox of his mortality, the poet catches the stare of the empiricist philosopher "Jack Locke," who moves steadily away from life's mystery represented by the buried lake. The poet, however, falls backward, his failures leading him into the empty music room and finally drowning in the lake, whose darkness becomes radiant with the presence of Saint Lucia. A pastoral scene is lighted through mirrors from the source of light which the poet is allowed to look upon only after his death. Finally, the dream ends, the illumination of divine light replacing the terror he had known in the headless corpse. The poet accomplishes a peaceful waking with the dream over, and he is for the first time certain of "enduring love" (*Collected Poems* 140).

In one of his later essays, "Our Cousin, Mr. Poe," Tate draws some further conclusions concerning the southern writer's relationship to the modern world. Poe's essential theme, Tate decides, is change. The effects of terror in "The Tell-Tale Heart" or "The Raven" symbolize the danger of aesthetic fragmentation, Poe's sense that the South's entrance into modernity via the slave system and the large-scale exportation of cotton was fraught with dangers to more than the economic order. Tate suggests that his own career parallels that of his "cousin" Poe, for they share an overwhelming sense of loss. Within the stable social order that Poe and Tate envisaged, the southern writer would fulfill the role of more than the modern "man of letters," the literary priest whose attempts partially filled the vacuum created by the lapse of belief in Christendom as a model of social order. Within the pre-modern order that Tate felt had been lost, the writer would recede into a secure anonymity, integrated within the larger social and spiritual order which his work would support. Unlike the modern writer, of whom Poe as the self-proclaimed master of the short story and fragmentary lyric is the perfect example, the pre-modern would receive an accessible body of myth from which to form an epic. According to Tate, Poe anticipated the reduction of modern writer to the "man of letters," the secular cleric working against the grain to arrest the inevitable decline of social order. The terror that one encounters in Poe's endings, and that one should find in Tate's as well, arises from the conviction that their societies are afflicted beyond the curative art of the man of letters. Lacking the "faith" of an Emerson, a faith based on the relinquishing of common experience to mechanism, the southern writer sensed disaster because he or she sought a connection between aesthetic order and common society.

Ultimately, Tate must have felt that he had resolved to some extent the problem of isolation of art from society that he had found symbolized in Poe's motifs of entombment and execution. The obsessive fear of "inevitable annihilation" which Tate notes as his "cousin's" central theme came to be a fundamental requirement of Tate's poetry, the desolation which confers authority to write of illumination and life, as well as of the inevitability of death. Tate believed that his generation had attempted to deal with mortality in escapist terms, through a display of material excess and technological power, and that its escapism was reflected in the abstraction and fragmentation of its art. The origins of this malaise could be specifically traced to nineteenth-century Romanticism, and writers such as Poe had sensed the approaching crisis. Tate believed, however, that his contemporaries had arrived at the crucial moment of collapse.

Thus, Allen Tate's attitudes toward modernity are distinctive among southern writers. No other, including William Faulkner, was able so clearly to place the contemporary situation within the context of historical development. Tate not only intuited but articulated the situation of his contemporaries, and he recognized the necessity for an aesthetic that would include and yet transform contemporary experience. That Tate felt a great deal of ambivalence about modernization in the South goes without saying, but unlike Davidson and Ransom he realized the need to incorporate modernity fully within his dialectic. In his poetry and criticism Allen Tate developed one of the most original responses to modernity in twentieth-century American writing.

Chapter 7

The Mechanical in *Everything That Rises Must Converge*

If Allen Tate had begun with a modernist aesthetic and subsequently formulated an aesthetic that tested the limits of Modernism, Flannery O'Connor would appear to be a writer who returned to conservative, even pre-modern responses to the changing South. For many readers, O'Connor's views on science and technology have been assumed to be an extension of an orthodox Catholic sensibility that found consummate illustration in the fundamentalism and social conservatism of a traditional culture. According to this interpretation, O'Connor perceived the new faith in science as the extension of a Post-Reformation reliance on Nominalism, a philosophical position that she never ceased to question. More damaging than pure science, the popular belief in technology as a panacea had led the twentieth century away from religious faith and toward belief in a future which enshrined technology. As Jane C. Keller insisted, O'Connor's empiricists had erected barriers between themselves and the recognition of the universe as the work of God (266). In the figure of Sheppard in "The Lame Shall Enter First," Thomas Carlson saw "the supreme exponent of Pelegianism," a character who "tries to render the material thing spiritual through technology, a kind of latter-day alchemy" (262).

Certainly O'Connor's writing might provide evidence for placing the treatment of mechanization in opposition to the religious message of her works. In a letter of March 17,1956, to Shirley Abbott, O'Connor expressed her rejection of a strictly empirical approach as she dismissed the popular view of science that confused objectivity with believing nothing. Only in the limited, laboratory setting does this view make sense. For the artist attempting to produce fiction "to believe nothing is to see nothing" (*Habit of Being* 147). Speaking of the sweeping impact of mechanization on the South and its effect on the southern writer, O'Connor remarked in "The Regional Writer" on the particular sense of uncertainty and doubt existing in the contemporary South. Presumably unlike the antebellum South, the modern South is a region of insecure identity where conventional values are questioned. Listening to the temper of this realistic analysis, one might well conclude that O'Connor's orthodox Catholicism, attested by her own statements and the majority of her critics, predisposed her to oppose the modern expansion of science and technology. According to this interpretation, modernization, as represented by a host of characters from Sheppard to Rayber to Mrs. McIntyre, may be interpreted as the object of satire in each of her works. The representation of the machine carries with it an implied negative cast, and the extent to which characters such as Mr. Head or Parker are depicted as "mechanical" indicates the working out of the destructive effects of a nominalist philosophy.

In view of the frequency with which this interpretation is repeated, it is striking to find that O'Connor had an extensive interest in natural and social science. While she implied at one point that science has led to the decline of Biblical knowledge and Bible reading (*Grace* 25), she admired Teilhard de Chardin as a scientist and a Christian, and in are view of his work, she spoke scathingly of "a caricature of Christianity. . . which sees human perfection as consisting in escape from the world and from nature" (*Grace* 87). As her book reviews indicate, O'Connor nurtured an open-minded interest in psychology; she praised *Cross Currents* for printing "the best that can be found on religious subjects as they impinge on the modern world, or on modern discoveries as they impinge on the Judeo-Christian tradition" (*Grace* 113).

One can trace the tension in O'Connor's writing between the traditionalist eager to decry the abuses of modernization, as when she describes the mass media as a "diet of fantasy" (*Grace* 86), and the sophisticated modern, aware of the latest advances in psychiatry and philosophy. One suspects that this internal struggle between traditionalist and modern underlies her comment singling out a quotation from Baron von Hugel: "'how thin and abstract,or how strained and inattentive, the religion of most women becomes, owing to their elimination of religious materials and divinely intended tensions!'" (*Grace* 21).

Though certain of her readers have sought to disregard the battling of"divinely intended tensions" in her writing, her fictional treatment of the changing South benefited enormously from her appreciation of the need to represent these tensions in her stories. The outright dismissal of mechanization would have resulted, as she recognized, in a very thin and "inattentive" body of fiction; more important to O'Connor, it would have mitigated against a clear-sighted application of religious truths to the modern world. O'Connor came to recognize that the predictable revulsion of the southern traditionalist to the "evil" of science was a failure of vision, a narrow-sighted disregard for the created world of sense experience. Her marginal lining of a passage in George Tavard's *Transience and Permanence: The Nature of Theology According to St. Bonaventure* highlighted the statement "that sense forms the first degree of the way to God and has thus a momentous religious value" (Kinney 46).

The emphasis of the concrete image as the starting point of vision is indeed fundamental in O'Connor's aesthetics, but the assumption that she arrived at this aesthetic position out of a deductive process of reading medieval exegesis or theology seems entirely inconsistent with what we know about the emergence of her narrative art. Rather, her reading in Catholic and non-Catholic theology, philosophy, and social science must have confirmed ideas on aesthetic practice that had already been formed long before any mature theological study occurred. Whether her recognition of the value of concrete writing was the result of the influence of the New Criticism, a movement that deeply marked her work, or was the working out of her own psychological needs during her narrative apprenticeship is a question that will probably be impossible to answer conclusively. That she was influenced by the ideas of Allen Tate and particularly by the advice of Caroline Gordon, that she had read a number of New Critical texts, and that she was trained in a school of writing which was emphatically New Critical can be demonstrated.

More pertinent to the issue of this study is the result of O'Connor's remarkable shaping of an aesthetic theory that insisted on fidelity to the naturalistic facts of the contemporary world while it sought to express supranaturalistic insights. O'Connor had been trained from the inception of her writing career in an aesthetic theory that excluded the rhetoric of transcendence, an aesthetic that William Faulkner only partially practiced and that Allen Tate worked toward throughout his career; in O'Connor's case the realistic bias in her aesthetic training conflicted with her intention to write a form of moral fable. From one perspective, one can see that Wise Blood is the perfect study of the Jamesian novel, written with strict control of the point of view and a density of specification that fell neatly within the New Critical understanding of Jamesian theory as interpreted by Percy Lubbock, and later by Cleanth Brooks, Robert Penn Warren, Wayne Booth, Mark Schorer, and others.

Nonetheless, in other respects O'Connor's first novel, *Wise Blood*, reveals intentions that fall outside this tradition, for while the technique of her writing, the careful limitation to the point of view of individualized characters and the accretion of specific details, is convincingly Jamesian, the larger shaping of her fiction is fairly subversive of the middle-class assumptions about motivation and behavior that are equally a part of the aesthetic of New Criticism and its understanding of literature. Without intending to downplay O'Connor's ultimate compassion for the Mrs. Mays of her fiction, one can see that the "secure" untroubled matrons and bachelors whose "faith" is grounded more than anything on illusive commonplaces of bourgeois language are the targets of her often virulent satire. Her character by and large is not the fully rounded "intelligence" whose consciousness is gradually revealed, but the representative figure closer to caricature. The Jamesian technique, predicated on the aesthetic assumption of complexity, only serves to exacerbate the sense of a debased idiom.

Furthermore, in an amazing strategy of aesthetic indirection, O'Connor has created fiction which ultimately confirms her friendless and isolated middle-aged heroines and heroes by insisting that their limitation is the basis of a spiritual search, a pattern that neatly parallels the dialectic of her aesthetic: with the legacy of a Jamesian aesthetic of self-effacement and limitation, O'Connor opens her fiction to the corrosive effects of satire and ambiguity, only to end with a seemingly more secure confirmation of her aesthetic origins. I would say "seemingly," because to many of her readers and perhaps to O'Connor herself, the interpretation of her fiction is clouded by psychological forces that tug in the opposite direction of her orthodox intention.

The issue of mechanization is crucial to this process of aesthetic reevaluation and formulation. Growing up in the post-war South at the point of its greatest industrial transformation and social change, O'Connor observed a radically different land from that of earlier southern writers. When Faulkner wrote of the machine, he still retained the agrarian ways very much in mind, if not as a viable future, at least as an experienced past. Almost all of his characters could remember with some nostalgia the agrarian pre-industrial South in which the automobile was a rarity. Even Allen Tate, who outlived O'Connor by fifteen years, grew up in a southern cultural milieu which was centered mythically if not actually in the agrarian past. For Flannery O'Connor and her generation, coming of age in the post-war South, the modernization of her region was a more compelling, inescapable reality. The grotesque transformation of the physical landscape of the South and the concurrent transfiguration of human manners and values became O'Connor's primary subject, and the enormous pressures of dealing with this material led to shifts in the aesthetic which O'Connor inherited from her predecessors.

With O'Connor the southern aesthetic for the first time fully reckoned with mechanization as the permanent and inescapable prospect of the region. Whatever theological fable O'Connor felt compelled to satisfy on the intentional level of her stories, the concrete reality out of which she writes is the fact of sweeping social and physical change with all the dislocation, destruction, and excitement it brings about. O'Connor is writing a fiction of "outrage," as Ihab Hassan recognizes, in which there is "a radical threat to man's nature" (240). In this post-modernist fiction, the sense of outrage arises not out of time, as it does in the writing of the Modernists but from space, so that the landscape itself becomes a metaphor for violence (Hassan 242).

Although the outrage of which Hassan writes is present in all O'Connor's books, the stories that comprise *Everything That Rises Must Converge*, written toward the end of her life, contain the greatest sense of a mechanical world. As several critics have noted, these stories center on the conflict between parents and children, a conflict, as Claire Katz states, that resembles the larger global struggle of technological society "to assert the magnitude of the individual against the engulfing enormity of a technological society which fragments social roles, shatters community, and splits off those qualities of warmth, intimacy and mutual dependence which nourish a sense of identity" (66). According to Katz, "the environment becomes a projection of sadistic impulses and fears" (61), yet there is no sense of any attempt or even wish to flee from the technological landscape. Instead, its sadistic power to corrode human feeling and to unveil illusions about the meaningfulness of human life is willingly embraced by the characters and by the author. The extent to which O'Connor relished the technological landscape is implied in her description of the New South as "a society that is rich in contradiction, rich in contrast, and particularly rich in its speech" (*Mystery and Manners* 103).

One might argue, as Katz has, that the nourishment that O'Connor received from the barren landscape of the New South is the result of a Freudian necessity to repress and violate the Ego: "Her peculiar insistence on absolute powerlessness as a condition of salvation so that any assertion of autonomy elicits violence with a vengeance. . . suggest[s] that at the center of her work is a psychological demand which overshadows her religious intent" (56). Despite the real perceptiveness of what Katz has to say, one can recognize the need for "absolute powerlessness," I think, without attributing it to a Freudian conflict. A separate argument may be made for the aesthetic necessity of representing the barrenness and powerlessness that the artist felt in the South's transition to modernity. The timing of O'Connor's arrival as a fiction writer required her participation in a southern literary tradition which had become dominated by New Criticism with its bias toward a Jamesian theory of narrative, yet her early adulthood coincided with the period of greatest technological change in the South. The Jamesian aesthetic with its gradual revelation of moral character and intricate play of sensibility against social context was hardly appropriate for recording the effects of mechanization on individuals who were overwhelmed by radical social and technological change. Thus, the outrage in the stories was not necessarily a projection of her need to experience violation: rather, O'Connor's fidelity to a naturalistic aesthetic reproduced the shock of the new with the same raw candor that Robert Frost had shown in such poems as "Home Burial" earlier in the century.

The post-war South in which O'Connor came to maturity was much changed from the South of Faulkner. Coming rapidly and resulting from outside pressures such as the New Deal programs of the thirties and the military spending of the forties, the southern experience of industrialization was different from that of the North, in which the industrial and urban experience was long familiar and of native origin. Certainly one would have to return to the writing of Emerson or Thoreau to find recorded the fresh sense of outrage with which the southerners of O'Connor's generation write of the machine, an outrage that helps to explain why the machine is so often associated with startling epiphanies at the end of her stories. Indeed, the "sadistic" landscape is the source of the "richest" humor, a paradoxical comedy that arises from our relief at admitting what we already know: that human beings are at times little more "human" than machines. In her treatment of the New South, the Faulknerian portrayal of the destruction of the wilderness or the ghastly rise of the Snopeses, almost always narrated from outside and with some nostalgia for the old older, is inconceivable because the distortions of landscape and social order brought about by mechanization are intrinsic to O'Connor's world. Also, the mechanical is so closely connected with the human condition as to make consciousness for any length of time unbearable without the recognition that one has been reduced to insensibility and repetition.

More fully than in either of her previous books, O'Connor presents an unremittingly mechanical world in *Everything That Rises Must Converge*. The shift toward the use of males as central intelligences may be connected with the intention to present the milieu of machinery and technological knowledge, although the farming operations of Mrs. May and Mrs. Turpin reflect a fully developed appreciation of the "benefits" of technology. If a maturing of O'Connor's aesthetic has taken place in this collection, as many readers believe it has, it is toward an appreciation of the potential artistic richness of the "barrenness" of technology. Her satire of mechanization is no longer as overtly funny as it had been in *Wise Blood* or *A Good Man Is Hard to Find* because O'Connor has meditated the distinction, raised by philosophers such as Jacques Maritain, between "Making" or productive action unrelated to the use of its product, and the modern sense of "making" as industrial production (Maritain 5-6). While Mrs. Turpin's pride in the cleanliness of her swine is certainly grotesque, but her understanding of the farming operation is not entirely determined by her narrow focus on technological means. Mrs. Turpin's appreciation of a certain coarse "aesthetic" of hog-farming, however comic it is made to seem by O'Connor's narrator, lies somewhere between the Scholasticist notion of use-less and the Modern use-ful forms of Action.

The best stories in this collection, among them "The Lame Shall Enter First," "Parker's Back," and "A View of the Woods," are equally unresolved: they lead us neither to embrace nor reject industrialization itself, but to smile at the absurdities of human responses to machines and to marvel at the ambiguities of the human condition in its fundamental mechanicalness. Carlson's reading of "Parker's Back," that "Parker intuitively grasps and rationally rejects . . . the union of spirit and matter, for the natural has no lasting meaning except to the degree that it is informed by the supernatural"(27), does not fully recognize that Parker's "search" is carried out *through* the mechanical world of the tattoo parlor and the pool hall. Certainly, the tattoo parlor has functioned aesthetically as more than "the false temple" (Carlson 270): it is the landscape that is somehow necessary to Parker's understanding of himself, a purgatorial setting where most of O'Connor's fiction transpires. Similarly, Mr. Fortune is more than "the modern fortune hunter, unable to accept nature for what she is rather than for what he can get out of her" (Carlson 258-59). By accepting the post-modernist landscape as her necessary canvas, O'Connor has recognized that to some extent the attitude of mechanized culture toward nature will always be "what he can get out of her" and this recognition has indelibly marked her aesthetic.

Even Sheppard of "The Lame Shall Enter First," certainly among the most "hopeless" of O'Connor's protagonists, reflects the maturity of her post-modernist aesthetic. Though we are tempted to label him as one of O'Connor's "intellectuals," an amoral ingenue who has fled the complexity of human suffering for a self-assured, complacent rationalization, Sheppard arrives at the most tragic sort of knowledge only *because* he has been seduced by the technological culture. His occupational specialization in testing, his belief that an IQ score measures the worth of a person, his faith that a special shoe, the product of medical technology, will bolster the image of a juvenile delinquent who sees the world as grotesquely evil: all these are examples of technological society's most fervid if inconsequential expressions of compassion. The gesture of making a telescope available to Rufus Johnson, while missing the point of the boy's real needs, is a sincere attempt to promote the child's growth.

The physical and social world is inherently "mechanical" to O'Connor, and Sheppard is beginning at the only possible point in the journey to self-understanding: that is, with immersion in the actual world of experience. Restricted to his own physical senses, inhibited by his hypersensitivity to touch and smell, Sheppard lives with a child who moves like a "mechanical toy" (*Stories* 378) and has taken on a delinquent rebel whose reflexive criminal acts assume no sense of freedom, an adolescent whose insults Sheppard describes accurately as "part of the boy's defensive mechanism" (*Stories* 383). Rufus Johnson is clearly a parody of the modern, a grotesque double of Sheppard himself, for he cynically advances the traditionalist religious rhetoric of his father only to further his own destructive whimsy. The point is that Rufus is the distortion of modernity, while Sheppard is the true modern, sincere in his intentions if uncertain of his direction. A rural transplant to the city who is cynical of "progress" but unable to live within the limitations of a pre-modern culture which his father's raw Fundamentalism requires, Rufus lives with a despair which is expressed in his comment to Norton that "'if you live long enough, you'll go to hell'" (*Stories* 462).

The major action of the story is Sheppard's gradual awakening to the mechanism of the world in which he lives, and the key symbol for this mechanism is the telescope. Unlike Rufus, who sees the telescope as a possession, an object of selfishness, and unlike Norton, who naively assumes that the instrument is the means to sight his lost mother, Sheppard feels that the telescope is a means of instruction. O'Connor's depiction of Sheppard as "instructor" is not altogether ironic, for he truly desires to teach Rufus and Norton about the future society in which they will live, even including the possibility of space travel, and his purchase of the telescope is intended to lead to a reformation of Rufus's character. O'Connor's hints that the telescope will lead to self-destruction do not diminish Sheppard's stature as a seeker of knowledge.

Sheppard's awakening to the limitations of his rationalist intellect originates during his visits to the brace shop, of which the description, like the symbolic interiors of Hawthorne's fiction, grimly symbolizes the human condition of suffering. Forced by the store clerk's complicitory wink to become an accomplice in fitting the shoe to Rufus's foot, Sheppard is struck by the accidental quality of human suffering and the extent to which the natural failing of the human body is intensified by the mechanical lack of feeling with which it is treated. "'In this shoe,'" the clerk comments, "'he won't know he don't have a normal foot'" (*Stories* 470).

Soon afterwards, Sheppard begins to see himself more accurately in the "distorting mirrors" of Rufus's eyes. Sheppard's own voice becomes increasingly mechanical, and his predictable efforts to save Rufus are now "involuntary," indications of a greater understanding of just how difficult the sort of freedom he seeks may be. What Sheppard begins to understand at the end of the story is the difficulty of maintaining his idealism, the moral sincerity that makes him more than an ironic "shepherd," at the same time that he participates fully in a modern technological culture, working with its necessarily limited possibilities for human freedom and creative action. He has not abandoned his quest to "reach for the stars," even on the night when he finds his only son hanging from the telescope which symbolizes belief in self-development. Instead, Sheppard has only arrived at the stage where his self-instruction has led to a merging of his positivist assumptions with a broader understanding of the future direction of human life. He has not worked "through" his faith in science but found that it coincides with acknowledge that transcends questions of immediate means. Sheppard's new understanding will never free him from the mechanical element in life, but it will lead to a compassionate appreciation in which the mechanical nature of life is the object of comic understanding.

Flannery O'Connor's definition of "southern" is itself informed by the sense of a culture in transition, as she observes in "The Regional Writer" that the identity of the South is "obscured" by the contemporary process of change. Surprisingly, perhaps, as she continues to note in the same essay, the South's history of defeat, of struggle, and of its present transformation all contribute in a positive way to the southern artist's "inburnt knowledge" of human nature and social reality. To be a southern writer is to look forward, toward a society in which nothing is static or secure, as well as backward toward a history which was no more stable than the present.

It is difficult to understand how readers attentive to what O'Connor actually says in *Mystery and Manners* could perceive her writing as nostalgic for the past or remote from contemporary reality. Louis D. Rubin argued some time ago that the dynamic tension behind O'Connor's creativity is the experience of living in a transitional culture, "exposed to several of the most revealing and dramatic contrasts of viewpoint and value possible to her time and place" (Rubin 50). The contrasts informing her fiction include fundamentalist religious belief, on which Rubin focuses, but also the increasing urbanization and mechanization of her region, and the changes in social values accompanying this transformation. O'Connor herself would assuredly have dismissed the notion that her stories are mere sociological representation of the New South, as she did in "The Nature and Aim of Fiction" in which she spoke of the absurdity of speaking of the "theme" of a story as "the economic pressure of the machine on the middle class" (*Mystery and Manners* 73). She would not, I believe, have dismissed the importance of social change as the setting and "matter" of her writing. She might well have admitted that the increasingly secular temper of her region, and its fascination with a newfound prosperity and sophistication, helped to determine the tenor of her satiric voice and the shape of her narrative.

O'Connor was drawn to this transitional landscape from the very beginning of her career, as the milieu of pullman cars, automobiles, urban boarding houses, theatres and diners in *Wise Blood* amply demonstrates. The stories of *A Good Man Is Hard to Find* are just as sharply focused on the marginal territory of city and country, modern and traditional, mechanical and agrarian. The automobile is so much more than an image in these stories: it is a dynamic and personified actor entering the stories as a comic and somewhat malevolent agent of personal freedom. Similarly, the setting of Rayber's home in *The Violent Bear It Away*, located in the post-war southern suburb, is examined satirically, even to the point, as Louis D. Rubin noted, of complaints against commercial breakfast cereal, yet this indictment of progress is incidental to the fundamental comic meaning which may be expressed as the eternally fallen and mechanical quality of human efforts. Whatever her personal antagonism (expressed often in letters and other commentaries) toward the New South's crass and repugnant manifestations of progress, her narrative truth is something broader than a lampoon of progress, for her writing is much more than a fiction of manners. Perhaps the extreme difficulty of portraying Rayber, which O'Connor complained of in her letters, has to do with not descending to a presentation of mere manners. In this case, O'Connor's discipline of mind and heart made it possible for her to avoid the temptation of deriding what she certainly found objectionable in her personal life, that is, to caricature Rayber as a modern acolyte of progress. O'Connor portrays Rayber as a mechanical man, one whose contacts with the world are filtered through a hearing aid, thick glasses, a sense of taste altered by a highly restricted diet, a sense of smell and touch limited by phobias of odor and human contact. Whatever the author's programmatic intentions in opposing Rayber the urban sociologist to Tarwater the rural fundamentalist, the depiction of Rayber creates at least some measure of sympathy.

As with many other characters in the fiction, including that of the Grandmother in "A Good Man Is Hard to Find," a certain undiscerning mechanicalness is associated with startling epiphanies during which the full recognition of loss appears. However, modernity is not the cause of this condition of loss but its anagogical symbol. The point is hardly that human beings such as Rayber have been reduced to acting mechanically because of the process of modernization in the South; for O'Connor humans have always resided in a condition of considerable ignorance in which their behavior is automatic, and one can point to examples of rural believers such as Mr. Head in "The Artificial Nigger" for whom this mechanicalness is as true as it is of Rayber.

Among the stories in *Everything That Rises Must Converge*, none is more concerned with the concept of mechanism than "Parker's Back." The story's setting is again the periphery demarcating rural tradition and urban modernism. After Parker's truck breaks down on the highway, he meets the provincial woman who will become his wife and whose disapproval of highways announces her withdrawal from the modern world. Retiring from the encroachment of machines, Sarah Ruth fears violation of her radically traditional world and so has no significant contact with modernity, while Parker stands out as the one character who is deeply disturbed by his own and others' qualities of mechanism. Parker cannot accept the gaze of his ancient employer who "looked at him the same way she looked at her old tractor" (*Complete Stories* 426), and with his complete lack of mechanical ability, Parker is more at odds with mechanization than others who reject it rhetorically.

The decisive moment comes when Parker stands, a country boy "heavy and earnest, ordinary as a loaf of bread" (*Complete Stories* 427) at the feet of a tattooed man at the fair and is filled with "unease" about his own existence. It is the possibility of an artificially and irreversibly "painted" body that disturbs him, for though his own dumpy, slow-moving body resembles the hulking battleship on which he serves, Parker's eyes suggest not mechanism but "mystery." Parker is entirely ill at ease in dealing with machinery, as his disabled car at the beginning of the story implies, and his urban forays are more attempts to repress the vocation of prophecy which his rural ancestors have prepared him for than they are meaningful inquiries for meaning in the city. Particularly it is the identity of Obadiah Elihue, the role of biblical prophet which he has not chosen, that he wishes to shift off by covering his body with tatoos of panther, lion, serpents, eagles, and hawks, all emblems of an aggressive modernism that he associates with the city. Tatoos impart a suggestion of urban sophistication and masculinity to his unimpressive frame, and Parker believes that tatoos are attractive to the country girls he meets.

Subconsciously Parker is drawn to choose the image of a Byzantine Christ, a tatoo which will cover his back (in both senses) and silence his overhearing wife. Instinctively Sarah Ruth understands Parker's defensive masculinity, and she misreads the fierce eagle on his skin for a domestic "chicken." More significant is her misprision of the

Byzantine Christ whose eyes burn from Parker's back, for she sees the portrait of Christ as idolatrous rather than the permanent emblem (something like the case of undine fever in "The Enduring Chill") of Parker's vocation as a prophet. Certainly it is significant that Sarah Ruth completely discounts the impulse that led Parker to take Christ "on his back," and likewise that she cowers from fear of a corrupt modernity, the world of pool halls and tatoo parlors that quite naturally attract Parker on his journey to become a prophet.

The "stern" and "all-demanding" quality of the Byzantine Christ compel Parker to select it from among a book of more contemporary religious illustrations (presumably innocuous portraits that would not have troubled Sarah Ruth upon his return home). By a neat inevitability the tattooed Christ lands on his back, for Parker has covered the front of his body with the less compelling modern emblems of animal force and carnality. Since Sarah Ruth has avoided confronting modern "defilement," which is in fact merely the lasting human condition in its current guise, it is understandable that she should misread as well the stern message of Parker's final tatoo. For Parker, however, the adoption of the Byzantine Christ is decisive. Driving at night across the rural landscape where he grew up, the country becomes "unfamiliar" after Parker begins his transformation into the prophet. The addition of eyes to the tattooed Christ on his back gives him the ability to see "backward" toward a religious tradition that antedated even Sarah Ruth's fundamentalist Protestantism. A final gesture of rebellion against his fate is the visit to a city poolroom lined with gambling machines, but Parker's rebellion is thwarted by the disturbing power of the Christ tatoo, which silences the men in the poolroom and leads to Parker's expulsion from the city. Ironically, the impulse to rid himself of the eyes of the prophet is identified with another, subconscious impulse to carry his new prophecy to the city. The glamorous urban decadence which he had once pursued becomes important now in another sense as a field prepared for his calling. When Parker flees to the "comfort" of his rural home, he finds ironically a less receptive response from Sarah Ruth than he found in the city poolroom.

Predictably, her narrow literalism finds the "Byzantine" Christ strange and idolatrous. Both city and country are inhospitable to his new prophecy, for the comfort that Parker associated with the country is a delusive trust in an assured, stable faith and in uncorrupted human nature.

The vision of progress in "A View of the Woods" again surveys the region's transition toward the industrial New South. Once again, the effort to portray the effects of this transformation mark O'Connor's aesthetic strategies more importantly than anything else in the story. By no means a"satire" of the New South or an attempt to suggest a return to the simpler ways of the agrarian life, the story succeeds aesthetically because it does not "promote" alternatives. It does, however, require the reader to move emotionally into the mechanical heart of the technological society and to replicate the spatial "barrenness" which the modern human condition has imposed.

Repetition, which Jacques Ellul pointed to as among the most significant features of every life in technological society, is a motif throughout the story from its early description of the digging machine, which would "gorge itself on clay, then with the sound of a deep sustained nausea and as low mechanical revulsion, turn and spit it up" (*Stories* 335), to the exact mirroring of the grandfather's face in Mary Fortune's. The persistent but ultimately unsuccessful effort of Mr. Fortune to comprehend modernity is the central action, for like many of O'Connor's works, the story traces the arrival of the southern countryman to modern culture. Fascinated by the machine and by the notion of "progress" which it represents (more awed of course than the sophisticated city dweller would be by these mechanical wonders), Mr. Fortune fails the other human beings around him, not because he has abandoned agrarianism for modernity, but because he has not understood modernity well enough. In an important sense, his failure is that he has not come far enough into the technological present. Like the protagonist of "Parker's Back" and other stories of rural immigrants to the city, Mr. Fortune clings inordinately to agrarian concepts of human free will and to sentimentalized ideas of human worth, illusions that have increasingly little application in an urban industrial South. Thinking that progress is his "ally" against a stubbornly independent son-in-law, Mr. Fortune plays into the hands of an enemy which he does not understand.

The sense of Mr. Fortune's misunderstanding of progress is paralleled by the larger community's clouding of the whole notion of urbanization. The fishing camp which is the basis for the new "town" of Fortune, Georgia, is the product of the urban misprision that the pastoral world provides a retreat from an urban workplace which is unlivable but unremediable. The comforts which city dwellers hope to find in the country are based on the pastoral illusion that the country offers a fundamentally simpler life than the city, a rehabilitative retreat for those who have suffered the cares of city life, a notion that O'Connor always dismissed with brisk irony. Like Sarah Ruth, the fundamentalist wife whose narrow demands of morality seem irresistibly attractive to the falsely nostalgic side of Parker, the rural southerner in O'Connor's tales is usually hypocritically attracted to the machine culture that he or she claims to despise.

Mr. Fortune is among the most significant of O'Connor's advocates of progress. Because he is essentially a countryman without real experience of industrialization, Mr. Fortune is all too susceptible to the allure of the machine, so much that he wishes to merge with it: sitting in his car with Mary's feet on his shoulders, he seemed "as if he were no more than a part of the automobile" (*Stories* 339). Despite this merging with the machine, he understands industrialization in a very imperfect way, for he sees it through the distorting lens of the myth of progress. Much as the railroad appeared to some nineteenth-century Americans, the bulldozer seems to Mr. Fortune the awe-inspiring savior. Mr. Fortune is one of those "afflicted with the doctrine of the perfectibility of human nature" that O'Connor describes in "The Teaching of Literature" (*Mystery and Manners* 133). As such, he is unusually disturbed by the "natural" fallenness of his son-in-law, whose beatings are inflicted inexplicably on his favorite granddaughter.

The crucial scene in the story is the beating which Mr. Fortune himself attempts to inflict on Mary. His granddaughter's violent resistance implies that the beating which he inflicts is of a different order than that administered by her father. In fact, Mr. Fortune intends to extract an admission that his granddaughter is a replication of his attitudes and behavior, that she is the exact product of his training. Significantly, he wishes Mary to subscribe to his faith in the myth of progress by repudiating her father's violence, yet Mary does not recognize her father's violence as "beating" because she understands that the human condition is inherently flawed, or in O'Connor's words that "a sense of loss is natural to us" (*Mystery and Manners* 133).

Coming of a later generation which is quite at home with mechanization and has seen its mark on the landscape with open eyes, Mary Fortune is willing to humor her grandfather's belief in progress up to the point when he decides to spoil the view of the woods by selling her father's cow pasture to erect a filling station. Although she can hardly have any sentimentalized notions of the nature of rural life, Mary insists on preserving the "view," the symbolic prospect which encompasses the changing landscape and through which she enjoys the vision of a transcendent value beyond the reach of a mechanistic philosophy. Even after the accidental killing his granddaughter, Mr. Fortune is still unable to grasp Mary's understanding of mechanism. The ironic ending of the story, with the rows of trees marching mechanically across the lake, implies that the need for a transcendent view evades Mr. Fortune even at the end of his life.

Mr. Fortune is consequently in a much worse condition than many of Flannery O'Connor's protagonists, because there is no recognition on his part of the myth of progress as a myth. Though it is in reality no "monster," the bulldozer appears as such to Mr. Fortune at the end because he has failed to humanize the machine by accepting it for what it is. He is still responding to the myth of the machine as savior, so the mechanical beating that he receives from his granddaughter ("five claws in the flesh of his upper arm where she was hanging from while her feet mechanically battered his knees and her free fist pounded him again and again in the chest" *Stories* 335) is the appropriate mirroring of his own distorting vision. To this limited extent he has managed to inscribe his self on another, the granddaughter who is his favorite only because she appears to acquiesce to his ideas.

Mr. Fortune becomes a truly grotesque figure not because he is the proponent of progress, but because he understands so little about the modern industrial culture. Understanding none of the larger psychic and emotional implications of technological society, he has adopted the machine as a kind of toy, and his taking Mary to watch the bulldozer dig up the earth reminds one of a childish sort of play. The extraordinary sadness of the story derives from the fact that Mr. Fortune is so much the product of an outdated generation that once exuberantly hailed the machine as the sign of a utopian age. In the modern South, Mr. Fortune is bound to be a lonely exponent of this enthusiasm.

In "A View of the Woods," O'Connor's purpose is not to satirize the industrialization of the South (a process that she may have deplored but did not spend herself campaigning against) but to explore the essentially mechanical element in human nature that is the source of all physical systems of mechanism. O'Connor understands that the denial of this source of mechanism in human nature or the attempt to refashion human nature is more damaging than the machine itself, which is the inevitable manifestation of the fallen condition. More important, mechanism plays a key role in O'Connor's comic aesthetic. The machine is not just a neutral force to be controlled by humane purposes: it is the most representative symbol for the repetitive, mechanical element in which human beings live most of the time. Typically, humans begin to resemble machines in this fiction, because, as the author views everyday life, the "normal" condition is in fact one of insensitivity and automatism.

However, if "mechanical" describes the normal condition of human society, it is also the basic trope in O'Connor's fictional aesthetic. To be "mechanical" is to be in a condition which, because of its imperfection, has the potential for the very qualities of warmth, humor, and compassion that originate in an awareness of lack; it is to be in a perpetual condition of need, just as Parker ("heavy and earnest, as ordinary as a loaf of bread") standing before the tattooed man at the fair feels a "peculiar unease" about "the fact that he existed" (*Stories* 427). Unlike the modernist generation of writers who by and large viewed the machine as a monstrous intrusion into the normal human society in which meaningful action was possible, O'Connor has depicted the mechanical level of reality as the primary and normative subject for her art.

Without detracting in any sense from the significance of O'Connor's accomplishment, one can understand that her fiction is the culmination of the efforts of southern writers such as Glasgow, Faulkner, and Tate to find ways of presenting an industrialized and urban South. The aesthetic tradition that O'Connor inherited and adapted in highly original ways meant that she was starting at a different point, aesthetically, in relation to the treatment of the machine than were earlier writers. The confidence and intellectual depth with which she approaches the subject reflect her own genius but also indicate how much she appropriated from the tortuous efforts of others to represent modernity as less alien and threatening than it had been to the Victorians and early modernists. When O'Connor arrived at artistic maturity following the Second World War, she found ways of using a southern landscape that had been literally transformed in the previous decade; she must have found even more useful those changes that had taken place in the southern aesthetic, which had then made available more realistic ways of representing change. In the work of those southerners who followed O'Connor, many of whom were chronologically her contemporaries, new experiments in dealing with technology would be forthcoming, yet not all those who followed achieved her remarkable understanding of the implications of change. In many respects O'Connor's fiction stands alone, even today, as the fruition of the modernist effort to represent change: as such, it is also the beginning of the post-modernist southern vision that is the starting point for such artists as Toni Morrison and Richard Ford.

Chapter 8

Art and the Mechanical in Styron's Fiction

In the many passages in which William Styron writes about war, a single motif dominates the writing. Briefly expressed, the idea is that since the First World World, the last major conflict which in the minds of the combatants could be imagined to be idealistic, modern warfare has become progressively mechanical and cynical. In this evolution the Second World War was pivotal, a transition from war that seemed purposeful and personal to war that was mechanical and meaningless. The soldier in World War II was in a position to look back to combat that was still fought primarily through infantry charges and at least preserved the trappings of "honorable" combat between individual opponents. In his essay "A Farewell to Arms" Styron could write that "the Pacific war may be viewed in retrospect as a discussible moral enterprise" (*Dust* 213), yet he could also sense, as did Norman Mailer, Joseph Heller, James Jones and others who wrote of the war, that the mechanical and "accidental" quality of the war was undermining the individual's sense of meaning. Furthermore, in the Pacific theatre the dignity of combat was reduced by the tendency on both sides to view the adversary in racist terms. Depicting the Japanese in sub-human terms, the American military reduced combat to mere "killing," a dehumanization that has multiplied in each of the Asian wars following World War II.

One anticipates that Styron will further explore this thesis in the forthcoming novel *The Way of a Warrior*. The sections that have appeared in serial format predict a novel in which a young Styron-surrogate is initiated into military experience that is losing its connection with the honorable past. However, if the war in the Pacific was brutal, Styron appears to preserve a good deal of nostalgia, if not for war itself (arriving at Okinawa just at the end of the war, Styron did not see combat), at least for the comaraderie of military life and the particularly severe and macho quality of Marine training, "that 'uncommon valor' of which the Marines are so justifiably proud" (*Dust* 216). If Styron is willing to grant that Vietnam was "an ignoble cause," he is equally adamant that the fundamental nature of military service is "moral" and that soldiers like Lt. William Calley have "disgraced" a calling that is otherwise honorable. Even in Vietnam he finds evidence "that in the midst of their most brutish activity there is a nobility in men that war itself cannot extinguish" (*Dust* 206).

At this point one must, I think, examine closely how Styron's writing distinguishes between the moral soldier "in the midst of. . . brutish activity" and a Lt. Calley at My Lai. What is it that separates the Marine of Styron's "good" war, removing the testicles from a slain "Jap," perceived as Styron himself declares in blatantly racist terms, from the "brutish" behavior of the latter-day Marine "pacifying" a Vietnamese village? War is Styron's microcosm for all human activity; the soldier, guilty by nature and brutalized further by experience, is his Everyman. If so, it is imperative to scrutinize the thesis of Styron's several essays on war, which is that the mechanical nature of modern experience has corrupted an enterprise that was once, and still may be potentially, ennobling as well as tragic. Is there really any difference between the conduct of war in our time and previous wars? Has war really become more impersonal, mechanical, and dehumanizing, or is Styron using the terms rhetorically, to argue that the nature of war itself is "moral"? By associating some contiguous aspects of Vietnam with the Second World War, does not Styron's writing intend to advance a revisionist view which would "alleviate the killing pain of [Vietnam], and its festering disgrace" (*Dust* 206)?

In addition to the question of historical revisionism, there is a more intriguing question concerning the connection of war and aesthetics. The most interesting aspect of Styron's analysis is his view that past wars have been redeemed through artistic representation, an assertion that should indicate his intention in dealing with the "festering disgrace" of Vietnam and with the inadequately represented Second World War as well. Ultimately, Styron presents an aesthetic argument which repeats in essence the modernist belief that artistic representation may recreate experience: if only we write well, the brutishness of events may be "alleviated."

Thus, there exists a connection between the morality of a particular war and the quality of writing occasioned by it. Styron writes: "It is possible, then, that the further we remove ourselves from wars in which a vestige of idealism exists. . . the less likely we are to produce imaginative writing that contains many plausible outlines of humanity" (*Dust* 204). A war which occasions great literature, as did the First World War, did so because the combatants were still idealistic enough to "believe" in the honor of their cause and in the "professionalism" of war itself. The decline of literature evidenced in World War II resulted from the corresponding decline of humanity on the part of the participants. The case *is* still out on Vietnam, but indications are that it produced no Hemingways or Wilfred Owens: from Styron's viewpoint, evidence of the increased "mechanicalness" of war. Since war is a reflection of broader cultural tendencies, the decline of "professionalism" in Vietnam reflects a general decline in American values: amateurism, mechanicalness, and disorder replace the civilized and professional conduct that one found in the military and in society at large before the Second World War.

Despite the pessimism of this reading, in Styron's view the case is still out on Vietnam and on World War II as well. The dramatic structure of each of his novels may be traced in these terms: Will the disorder of the present or recent past be assuaged by the accomplishment of the artist which the present awaits? Will the artist succeed in recreating experience which by itself is incomprehensible? If there is abundant evidence of modern decline, there is also hope that the artist will assuage the pain of events by writing of them with the same professionalism that Styron sees in the military careerism of the past. Clearly, in pronouncing Ronald J. Glasser's *365 Days* "a valuable and redemptive work" Styron has implied that even the Vietnam experience is redeemable because it has been written about well: he has indeed adopted an aesthetic argument that the fundamental reality of events is recreated by the artist's representation, and that even the pressing and horrible event possesses no meaningful reality until given representation by the author.

Styron's earlier work indicates that he has always held a strongly ambivalent view of war, indeed, an ambivalence which extends to all areas of human experience that one would ordinarily term "evil" or destructive. John Crane has written that the design of Styron's work lies in the redemptive confrontation of evil, a reading that does seem to clarify the structural pattern of the novels, but that also increases the troubling sense that Styron has dismissed the nightmares of war, racism, and holocaust by means of an aesthetic purgation in which the role of the artist-as-creator is pivotal. No less than in his more recent treatments of evil, *The Long March* is an effort to apply an essentially modernist vision to historical events that may not be "redeemable."

The redemption which one finds in Styron's treatments of war is not the psychological or cathartic sort that Crane outlines, nor is it the religious or specifically Christian salvation that some have perceived and that Styron himself invites with rather frequent nods to critics bent on reading religious patterns and symbols in his work. As his nostalgia for the pre-modern idealism of war proves, Styron offers no indication that human society before the contemporary period required redemption: if as recently as the Second World War the soldier could undertake killing, even of the hellish sort carried out in the Pacific theatre, with a sense of idealism, what must Styron think of those earlier wars in which the combatants more or less attempted to avoid the killing of civilians and fought by some sense of rule of honor? (Even the history of slavery, as one learns in *The*

Confessions of Nat Turner, does not in Styron's mind constitute evidence of a universal dehumanization, only a past scattered with brutal exceptions.) It seems evident that in Styron's view real brutality is limited to contemporary experience, that even in the contemporary nightmare, evil can co-exist with humane and idealistic gestures, and that even this evil can be "alleviated" by writing (and reading) about it. While these beliefs argue in favor of a modernist aesthetic with its emphasis on artistic re-creation, they also argue against any view of experience that may with assurance be located within the mainstream of Christian theological tradition.

A more insistent element of the fiction is the assertion of "tragedy" as an aesthetic form which aims at the effect of catharsis. The source for Styron's conception of tragedy may be European existentialism rather than Greek classicism, and the novels contain evidence of close familiarity with the entire tradition of the literature of alienation from Dostoevsky to Sartre. Underlying the structure of *The Confessions of Nat Turner* is the influence of Camus' *The Stranger,* in which a prisoner on trial for an apparently absurd murder reviews the events of his life and comes to an existentialist acceptance of responsibility for the present. Styron turns this structure to quite another purpose, ending his novel with the hand of Thomas Gray reaching through Nat's cell, a moment of human recognition between apparent opposites, and with Gray gaining a sense of humanity from Nat's sacrificial death (somewhat as the community of Jefferson does from the brutal lynching of Joe Christmas in Faulkner's *Light in August*). In fact none of Styron's novels ends with a truly existentialist understanding, although the author has skillfully absorbed and at many points parodied the style of the existentialist novel. Rather, the most revealing influence on Styron's tragic art is the Anglo-American tradition of Modernism, with its romantic transcendence of ordinary reality through the figure of the artist-as-creator.

In this aesthetic tradition, particularly as practiced by American authors, the experience of tragedy takes place in the mind of a solitary Ishmael, pondering the monstrous events from a distance that replicates the artist's separation from everyday life. Because the writer is always a solitary artist, the catharsis of such tragedy comes more as a private resolution than a communal experience, a private catharsis rather than a prophetic vision with social consequences outside the individual consciousness. Styron's artistic self-consciousness, the fact that his fictions are highly literary works written in a sense as parody of the conventions, including the conventions of the southern novel and of Faulkner's work itself, does not alter the fact that his novels do not move beyond earlier assumptions about the relationship of artist to subject. Despite the high degree of self-conscious artistry with which he constructs his novels, framing the novel with artful narrators and undercutting the narrators themselves by ironies of tone and structure, Styron's essential view of the relationship of art to world does not move beyond modernist assumptions, for the artist, even though masked behind layers of self-parody and artifice, remains committed to re-creating the insufficient world of experience.

The treatment of the military in *The Long March* illustrates these generalizations. Set during the Korean War, the novel is curiously enough a "war story" that does not really depict war. The recruits in the novel are reservists rather than career military and are thus in an ambivalent relationship to military life from the beginning. The very "given" of the fiction intentionally complicates the examination of its apparent subject, the mechanical nature of military training and the brutalizing effect of military life (taken as a microcosm of life in general). The first narrated event, the death of eight soldiers struck at mess by a stray mortar round, bears the accidental quality of a traffic fatality rather than the intentional destructiveness of war. Styron relieves the narration of a sense of real suffering in this passage by calling the soldiers "boys," as if they were playing at death, and later by having Culver reflect that the "eight dead boys" had never understood the immensity of pain in the world and thus had never felt "the tender miracle of pity" (116).

From the beginning, then, a peculiarly ambivalent treatment is applied to the matter of military training and by extention to the broader issue of human suffering in general. If the eight mortar victims are not really conscious of the human condition of suffering, neither is the military system of which they were a part. Although one supposes that much of the suffering in the story might be traced directly to the sadistic Colonel Templeton, *Culver* realizes that the officers are also victims of an impersonal machine. In a paradoxical sense Templeton is more innocent than others because he has been conditioned by a lifetime of military discipline which has induced a reflexive submissiveness to authority. The description of Templeton captures perfectly Styron's own ambivalence. Once he has ordered the thirty-six mile march, the Colonel "pushed ahead in front of [Culver] with the absolute mechanical confidence of a wound-up, strutting tin soldier on a table top" (74). Observing the Colonel as he strokes Mannix's swollen foot, Culver concludes that "he had too long been conditioned by the system to perform with grace a human act" (89).

Another paradox would seem to be that Captain Mannix, the rebellious protagonist who in many ways resembles Albert Camus' existentialist hero, becomes more mechanical and sadistic than the Colonel he opposes. Foreshadowing Nathan Landau, another rebel driven mad by the injustice that obsesses him, Mannix's righteous opposition is more destructive than the authority of the Colonel, who leaves the recruits an "out" of riding back to the base. Mannix's determination to complete the march, and to have his platoon complete it, is linked to his unconscious admiration of, and participation in, the very human domination that he deplores. "In the midst of his pain," Culver says, Mannix "yeild[s] up still only words of accord and respect and even admiration for the creator of such a wild and lunatic punishment" (101). This passage suggests rather clearly that the victim participates in the act of victimization, and that rebellion lacks meaning without the existence of an oppressor. Indeed, Culver approaches the knowledge that the reservists are really just as much marines as the robotic grunts they ridicule, that in fact Mannix in his rebellion is more "marine" than O'Leary, the easy-going lifer whose loyalty to the chain of command is automatic and thus innocent. As Culver comes to see, O'Leary, Mannix, and Culver himself "had been marines, it seemed, all their lives, would go on being marines forever" (102-3).

In addition, there is an insistence that all actors in the story are equally and absolutely guilty: all except one, the artist-figure Culver, who does experience "the tender miracle of pity" and who longs for serenity, a state that he connects with music, as an escape from the brutality of a world reduced to system. Admittedly, Mannix's rebellion originates in a humane impulse to oppose victimization, but it is Culver and not Mannix who experiences the recognition of guilt and pity at the end of the novel. No matter how idealistic his motives (indeed, because of his idealism) Mannix becomes co-opted by the system. Colonel Templeton does not really expect "B" Company to complete the march; his purpose is only to establish reflexive authority over the new recruits. By defying the Colonel, Captain Mannix establishes military discipline more effec-tively than the Colonel could ever have done. The novel implies that direct engagement of the system does not lessen its power, but that such rebellion, the fundamental act of existentialist good faith, increases the oppression. Rather, as is suggested by the key position of the narrator as a disengaged observer, the mechanical suffering of the human condition is redeemed by aesthetic means.

The connection of aesthetics and human suffering is made explicitly as Culver defines the relationship between two essential and related features of the human condition, suffering and exaltation. Suffering includes not only the physical torment of Mannix trudging six miles with a nail in his boot and completing the remaining thirty miles on a swollen foot, but also his emotional anguish at the deaths of the eight "boys" and his outrage at the Colonel's blind cruelty. Exaltation derives from a consciousness of evil and from a shared understanding of the condition of suffering. For "one unspoken moment of sympathy and understanding" (120) Mannix experiences this exaltation in the presence of a Negro maid, before whom he stands naked and scarred. Nonetheless, it is really left to Culver to experience serenity and to shape a cathartic expression of what he has learned. As for Mannix, he is doomed to an uncertain future with Colonel Templeton's threat of a court-marshall and transfer to Korea hanging over his head. The immediate and more pressing question of Mannix's foot remains, which in neat symbolism is left without medical attention, along with the impending storm which never arrives.

In *Sophie's Choice* William Styron approaches the theme of evil on a much larger scale than in *The Long March*, but the importance of aesthetics as a response to evil is similar. The nightmare of the Holocaust should be understood as a form of mechanicalness of man toward man, an application of "technique" to the task of killing which Styron also saw underlying the massacre at My Lai. However, the mechanism of history is not only ghastly and "monstrous," a word which is applied most often to the Hoss household but also rather often to Nathan Landau and to Sophie's father, Professor Zawistowska, but also necessary in certain ways. Again, according to John Crane the "solution" to the problem of evil appears to lie in a catharsis which forces a confrontation with and an admission of the the human attraction to evil. Avoidance of this confrontation only results in a multiplication of evil, a complacent involvement in actions for which one refuses responsibility. It is, however, debatable as to whether in the novel the representations of mechanism of all sorts, and centrally of the great mechanism of the death camps, do in fact accomplish this purgation, and if a cathartic scene does appear at the end with "morning, excellent and fair" and with Stingo, Lazarus-like, emerging from burial in the sand. For many readers the ending appears tagged on to the overwhelming horror that has preceded it. Nonetheless, the novel does contain a powerful representation of evil, a revelation of guilt and inhumanity that convinces despite the questionable resolution.

One source of guilt is the survival of the narrator who "lives to tell," the Styron/Stingo, Styron/Thomas Gray, Styron/Peter Leverett whose guilt results from the very fact that he has survived while others have not. More is revealed, however, than the psychological affliction of the survivor, for the autobiographical narrators are guilty in more direct ways of complacency and insensitivity, aesthetic inattentiveness that is indeed monstrous. Beyond this there is a sense of guilt that arises from fictionalizing what may remain, despite the artist's purgatory of craft and artistic perfection of meaning, an untranslatable experience of horror from contemporary history. The author has selected a subject of such overwhleming historical reality that many reviewers have questioned Styron's assumption that the Holocaust was not a unique historical event, beyond fictionalizing and certainly beyond the narrative purview of an adolescent Stingo (however much later the story is assumed to have been penned by the mature Stingo). It is illuminating to contrast Styron's treatment to that of Jewish writers such as Uri Zvi Greenberg, whose poem "To God in Europe" typifies the sense of many Jewish authors and survivers that the Holocaust had shattered any meaningful connection with the past. Of the treatment of his people by Gentiles, Greenberg writes: "Where are there instances of catastrophe/ like this that we have suffered at their hands?/ There are none" (Roskies 575). In contrast Styron asserts that the Holocaust is an extention of the universal sufferings of common existence, in some way comparable to the record of American slavery or the treatment of Poles such as Sophie at the hands of the Nazis. The larger events of history are indeed comprehensible to the individual, but only after they are re-created by the artist.

For the actual description of Auschwitz, Styron relies on documentary evidence, including the testimony of Commandant Hoss to the enormity of the logistical and technical problems involved in carrying out genocide on such a scale. The Jews and others are victims of a monstrous mechanism, a machine for killing for which the systematic and disciplined Hoss is the appropriate agent. The emphasis on Auschwitz-as-mechanism, however, deflects analysis from the suffering of victims and the responsibility of victimizers, just as the portrait of Hoss as an overwhelmed bureaucrat, one who wishes he had never heard of the Final Solution but struggles to carry it out, blurs the distinction between brutal murderer and mere technician.

Essentially, Styron carries on the modernist critique of the machine in which objective reality is transformed by the overwhelming power of mechanism and the pervasiveness of technique, Ellul's sense of technique as organic and uncontrollable, while the artist gains control of a separate private reality through aesthetic creation. Attitudes toward the machine that Allen Tate examined and rejected in his critique of Matthew Arnold are revived in Styron's somewhat melodramatic representation. The key word in this presentation since *Set This House on Fire* has been "monstrous," and its function is to label the radically mechanical nature of modern experience as "evil" beyond examination. The modernist shudder of horror at the expanding power of the machine itself is extended in the postwar period to the mystique of bureaucracy and technical expertise, the expansion of social organization and the emergence of the computer as a means of social control. One subtext of *Sophie's Choice* is the familiar post-war metaphor of a human being as "only a number," an instance of the novel's general strategy of establishing identification between the Holocaust and universal experience.

The artistic problem may be illustrated by focusing on the treatment of Sophie Zawistowska. It is not coincidental that among the many critical treatments of the novel, few have centered on what is ostensibly its "central" figure. Most have dealt in more detail with Stingo as a representation of Styron, or with the treatment of the Holocaust itself. Nonetheless, I believe that Styron intended Sophie as the novel's center and her death as tragedy. To accept the centrality of her position, however, necessitates the admission of certain assumptions about modernity, the most important of which is not merely the inevitable mechanicalness of human nature but the impossibility of alieviating its effect except through art. Further, while the mechanical aspect of experience is terrifying, in the author's view it is apparently purifying as an experience that leads to a state of meditation that is analogous to music: it is the ordeal which the marine-as-everyman confronts and endures, and which is followed by an emotional condition of peace.

As emotionally compelling as the narrative may be, in this depiction there is little sense of a realistic effort to "illuminate" the sources of the Holocaust so that mankind's primitive sympathy with violence is brought to examination. While Styron indisputably captures some of the horror of the events by drawing on historical accounts of the concentration camps, his fictional treatment of the main victim Sophie remains clouded, as it must if one is to apply the modernist critique to events of such contemporary ethical importance. Ultimately in this novel Sophie plays out her role as victim and the novel's resolution reverts to the consciousness of the artist-figure. The fact that Stingo speaks of the difficulty of comprehending Sophie's life, that he may never fully understand the events he narrates, does not change his fundamental relationship to the events. The most horrifying fact of the novel is that ultimately the Holocaust is significant to Stingo as an aesthetic rather than a political event. The meaning of Sophie and Nathan's lives is finally that Stingo must comprehend them as an *artist*.

Because the point of view is essentially modernist, mechanization is associated with several familiar motifs. As one finds in Faulkner's treatment of aviation, the suggestion of sexual promiscuity is never far removed from the depiction of machines, which are potent themselves and arouse those humans who work close to them. Whether she merits it or not, in Stingo's imagination Sophie is not only the model of the experienced older woman but also representative of European sophistication: on both counts she is threatening and enticing at the same time. Stingo is never able to distinguish the human Sophie from the Sophie of his imagination, and this is particularly the case in the cathartic ending after her and Nathan's deaths. Enormously insensitive to the dehumanization to which Sophie has been subjected, Stingo is determined to make her a part of his work, of which the present novel is represented as the product.

Since the author is aware of this victimization, there is a good deal of self-mockery in his portrait of Stingo as youthful Styron. Nonetheless, concerning the most significant facet of Stingo's character, his determination to view the world as a modernist artist, the intention does not appear to be ironic. Despite the satire with which he depicts Stingo's naive ambition to write the Great American Novel, Styron's more self-conscious and far more subtle artistry submits to the modernist ambition to salvage historical experience through artistic creation. The more obvious political solutions to injustice and inhumanity are not advanced, and one is left with a vaguely classical sense that life is irremediably tragic. The countless scenes in which Sophie is violated in mechanical ways, both by the Nazis in Europe and by Americans including Nathan and Stingo, leave the reader with a frustrated and angry sense of her helplessness. The further suggestion that after her losses at Auschwitz she almost wishes to die, and that even before the camps she invited violation by powerful males, raises questions about the characterization of Sophie. Some early reviewers of the novel objected that the central representative of the Holocaust was not Jewish: given Sophie's charater, would they not have been more outraged if she *had* been?

The novel's purpose, however, is to suggest that guilt is universal and "ultimately beyond expiation" (*Sophie's Choice* 361). Since all readers share this guilt, all are in need of the catharsis which the novel provides, and the novel itself is the "solution" to the problem of guilt. Although it can never be "expiated," guilt can be assuaged, at least momentarily. Few modern writers have as effectively represented this theme, the universality of guilt and the anguish of those who carry the burden of guilt. Like Flannery O'Connor to an extent, William Styron writes of the limitations of human nature and the problem of evil: the social and psychological world in Styron's fiction is scarred by a history of victimization, and both victim and victimizer, who may reside in one person, seek peace and refuge.

If the diagnosis of evil is similar in the fiction Styron and O'Connor, the suggested "solutions" are quite different. In William Styron's fiction, whether in the case of Culver, Peter Leverett, Thomas R. Gray, Nat Turner, or Stingo, the narrative consciousness comes across as that of the aesthete: detached, morally indecisive or ambiguous, more interested in aesthetics than life. The narrator is self-creative, and the events of the fiction ultimately lack ontological reality except in that they are re-created by the narrator. The ambitious task of this fiction is to apply the modernist aesthetic to the most troubling, immoral events of modern history; the sadness of narrators such as Stingo and Culver is related to the fact that their youthful ambition, to make sense of the world through abstract theories of beauty or justice, is overwhelmed by the harsh reality of history.

The Holocaust has occupied Styron for much of his career, with many scenes in the novels preceeding *Sophie's Choice* anticipating its full-scale treatment. For instance, in *Set This House on Fire* Cass Kinsolving's dream of watching himself suffocate in the gas chambers involves a number of elements that would be expanded in *Sophie's Choice*. The scene is accompanied by music, "a discordant, atonal sound as of some bizarre ensemble playing off-key yet in unison" (374). There is the suggestion of sexual arousal accompanying Cass' death, for seeing his naked body, a "ripe mulatto girl" shrieks "as if to obliterate the sight not just from her own eyes but from all eyes" (375). Styron is removed four times from his subject, for one reads the account through Styron, who derives it from Peter Leverett, who takes it from Cass, who watches the "other" Cass of his dream. Also, Cass says that he awoke "blotting out the message from his mind even as he awoke" (375), an anticipation of the surprisingly untroubled awakening of Stingo after Sophie's death.

The racial holocaust represented in *The Confessions of Nat Turner* is associated with similar elements and narrated in a similar style. Upon entering the fast which preceeds his revolt, Nat is beseiged by "devils and monsters," in particular by the image of a sensual Negro girl whom he has noticed in town (330). Like the temptress in his dream, the single victim at Nat's hands, Margaret Whitehead, is also the object of his "remorseless desire" (353-54). Nat prepares his plans for the revolt during his solitary retreats in the woods, during which he enters a state of meditation that Styron elsewhere identifies with music. (Nat knows by heart the Psalms of David, which he recites often during the workday.) Nat's story is told at several removes through the intermediary of Thomas Gray, an intriguing double of Styron. Even more significant is the fact of Nat's alienation, not only from the whites but also from all but one of the blacks whom he leads. Even in the case of Hark, his closest associate, Nat's friendship takes the alienating form at once of friendly patronization and stern command.

Styron's Nat Turner is a detached observer, re-creating the world through his inventive consciousness in the same way that Faulkner's modernist narrators imagine reality. When the killing is actually carried out, Nat's impulse is to turn back or turn away rather than look squarely at the product of his imagination. The narrator Thomas Gray is essentially sympathetic to Nat, despite his racial badgering and legalistic reserve, and Gray's morally ambiguous conclusion is Nat's as well. Rather than reaching any final assessment of the events, Gray's conclusion is "the hope of being what I could be for a time" (510). If this seems like less than enought for a novel filled with extraordinary violence, it is because the real resolution is aesthetic, not ethical. The holocausts of Styron's fiction are significant as aesthetic objects but not as historical events with actual physical consequences. Repeatedly the significance of mechanism in Styron's fiction is its immense and expanding force, which the artist responds to with private acts of catharsis and joy.

The victimization of Sophie is the most elaborate example of this aesthetic response to mechanism. It is important to recognize the structural design in which Sophie's character has a part, for Sophie's victimization is necessary for the enlargement of the force of mechanism, which functions in the novel's design as an antagonist to the artist-figure Stingo, who is the actual protagonist. If one accepts the fictional aesthetic under which Styron is writing, which is a modernist aesthetic that would have been appropriate to Faulkner, one finds the resolutions fully satisfactory, for in these endings the protagonist/artist has succeeded in rendering evil in an ordered structure, an epic comedy in which the most horrible events point toward illumination and peace.

However, for this design to succeed, characters such as Sophie or Mannix must be sacrificed to the monstrous power of that mechanism which the author struggles to comprehend. Those critics who have objected to the passivity of Sophie's character, her apparently masochistic willingness to be dominated by all sadistic males (and not only by males), have not understood Styron's intention. Ultimately, none of his victims are permitted to rise as willful individuals because Styron has taken as his premise that the overwhelming force of evil (call it mechanism, modern history or human nature) will defeat the world until it is re-created by the authorial imagination. Thus, Sophie's final destruction, the event that seals her doom long before her actual death, is the choice forced upon her by the "Christian" Doctor Jemand von Niemand, the faith-seeking everyman who perfectly represents Styron's despair with the actual world and his hopefulness of a resolution in the transcendent realm of art.

Each of Styron's tragic victims acquiesces in his or her victimization because he or she senses the superhuman power of the mechanical. From the beginning of her life Sophie reads the inflexible figure of her scholar-father into all the males whom she meets or even dreams about. When she finds a lover who is not sadistic, in the person of Stingo, she finds him "cute" but insignificant, unable to project the same authority as her mechanical father, and deserts him on their pre-marital "honeymoon." With Sophie's masochism the author presents a vision of a universe of characters who carry guilt beyond expiation and who invite a universe of monstrous violence, though through their crucified lives they bring understanding to their survivors.

These tragic protagonists, whose victimization is drawn with great artistic power and toward whom Styron is deeply compassionate, finish by acquiescing too readily in their victimization. Mannix, for example, insists on his role as victim, as if he were eagerly pursuing a well-deserved punishment from the father-like Col. Templeton. Nat Turner, after the collapse of his slave revolt and at the point where the narrative begins, readily assumes the role of victim to the enraged and frightened white society. Sophie's near grovelling to all male authority is yet another example of this tendency for Styron's victims to acquiese in their punishment. As the narrative commentary makes clear, all three tragic characters share in the "guilt" of the inhumane system which victimizes them. Mannix had "always" been a soldier; Nat Turner patronized other blacks with an arrogant egotism that mimicked white prejudices toward blacks; Sophie collaborated in the Holocaust, typing the manuscripts of her father's antisemitic articles and working as secretary for Herr Hoss. Each of these characters acquiesces because he or she shares in the nature of evil, living in a state of apathy or self-absorption. From the beginning of her life, Sophie for example reads the inflexible figure of her father, to whose discipline she seems pathologically subservient, into all the males she meets or even dreams about: not only is she habitually passive toward assertive males, but she appears to enjoy, even on an erotic level, contact with dominating males. Nat Turner, it might be noted, responds to the same sense of social privilege which underlies the freedoms which Margaret Whitehead boldly takes with him, appearing before him in her underclothes as she would before no white male, brushing against his body during a carriage ride, and demanding responses to personal questions that a slave cannot allow himself to answer.

The extent to which Styron relies on aesthetics as a means of resolving the problem of universal participation in evil is indicated by the association of evil and faulty communication in *Sophie's Choice*. Stingo moves through a world in which the worst violations are carried out wordlessly and in silence. Of course, the most memorable example is the silence in which Sophie from her distant post observes the division of prisoners on the quay at Auschwitz, but lesser silences pervade the novel, anticipating and echoing the central instance of Auschwitz. A busload of Jewish deaf mutes rides with Sophie and Stingo to Jones' Beach, causing Stingo to anticipate the final catastrophe of Sophie's death (*Sophie's Choice* 427-8). Stingo's father notes the decline of manners and "conversation" in the barbarian North after his confrontation with a New York cabbie (*Sophie's*

Choice 355-7), while the southern racist Bilbo dies, ironically, of cancer of the mouth. For Stingo and Sophie sex is "a kind of furious obsessed wordlessness finally" (*Sophie's Choice* 604), though whether with Sophie or with his other partners, the linguistic prude Mary Alice Grimball or the totally lingual Leslie Lapidus, eros for Stingo is stoney and grim. What Stingo takes to be an initiation to marital bliss is for the desolate Sophie the silent, hopeless end of life.

The artist's task, Styron has stated, is to achieve a level of expression that counters the clumsy or non-existent communication of the "real" world. Styron rarely presents artist personae without parody, as in the ironic self-portrait of Stingo's discourse on the peanut, which he asserts is "the appropriate commonplace out of which to refashion new conduits of communication" (*Sophie's Choice* 594), and which follows close upon Sophie's disclosure of her ultimate ordeal at Auschwitz. The bumptious Stingo, who claims that "on rare occasions, when the moment is exactly right and the audience is utterly responsive, my encyclopedic ability to run on and on about a subject has served me in good stead," is surely a parodic inversion of the "true" artist, who is neither didactic nor concerned with "useless facts and empty statistics" (*Sophie's Choice* 594). Likewise, Stingo's repeated apologies for "extraneous stuff" (*Sophie's Choice* 143) or passages which "might be considered unnecessary to recount" (*Sophie's Choice* 376) disguise somewhat coyly the novel's carefully wrought structure.

While Styron may parody the apprentice artist with his claims of "encyclopedic ability," he nonetheless asserts a narrative aesthetic in which the artist takes on a central role as he or she re-creates experience in response to the universal mechanism found in the actual world. Styron's treatment of mechanization is similar to that of the Modernists in turning from modernization to aesthetics. With the modern world seen as increasingly monstrous as it becomes more efficient and mechanized, the artist turns to a modernist aesthetics of fiction emphasizing technique and the artist's creation of an aesthetic realm as an alternative to commonplace reality. The world is "redeemed" by the artist re-creating it, but the increasing force of inhuman mechanisms of victimization remains, like all human crimes, ultimately beyond expression.

Chapter 9

Ernest Gaines and the New South

Although the imaginative setting of Ernest Gaines' stories is little more than a hundred miles removed from the Feliciana Parish of Walker Percy's fiction, and though Gaines and Percy began published first novels within three years of one another, the disparities in treatment of the New South by these two writers are remarkable. Unlike the fiction of Walker Percy, which as we shall see in many essential respects returns to Agrarian modes of thinking about the machine, the works of Ernest Gaines couple a highly realistic depiction of technological change with an insistence on the value of connection with the past and the responsibility of the individual to communal needs.

Ernest Gaines began his career as a novelist in the late fifties, a period of turbulent social protest and unprecedented economic progress in the South. The issues of social and economic change are clearly in the forefront of Gaines' fiction, a fact which a number of commentators have stressed. However, the diversity of critical opinion concerning the treatment of change in Gaines' fiction invites a more detailed study of the author's view of the New South, and of the participation of blacks in the post-war boom in the region.

As a subject of fiction the New South has occupied Gaines' attention from the beginning of his career up to the present, as a detailed analysis of two of his works, the early collection of stories *Bloodline* and the later novel, *In My Father's House*, will demonstrate.

Furthermore, as in the case of Flannery O'Connor and other post-war southern writers, Gaines' fictional treatment of the New South has affected his narrative aesthetic. The distinctive features of prose style and technique in his fiction have evolved, at least in part, by the necessity of representing the subject of social and economic change. Where Gaines is most innovative, in the subtle effects of voice and point of view, he is often dealing directly with the impact of social and technological change on his rural Louisiana setting. Gaines also resembles O'Connor in the extent to which he has appropriated a highly developed southern literary tradition which suggests conventional responses to mechanization. There are important echoes as well of the major black writers, especially Charles Chesnutt and Richard Wright, who wrote into their works an offer bitterly ironic response to the "New" South. Gaines' accomplishment may well be to have brought together a black literary tradition, with its emphasis on ironic commentary and folkloric material, and the southern literary aesthetic of Glasgow, Faulkner, and O'Connor.

Historians such as George Tindall, John Hope Franklin, and Gavin Wright have documented the extent of social change in the post-war South, pointing to New Deal policies and war-time expenditures, as major factors in changing economic and social attitudes. The location of military bases in the Deep South provided new contact with thousands of soldiers from outside the region and provided the impetus for growth in such cities as Mobile and Norfolk. Despite a limited amount of integration within the services, military service opened up new skills and experiences for black enlisted men. Equally important, with 17.6 percent of the total expenditure for war plants going to the South, southern cities were rapidly transformed into industrial centers, and the phenomenal post-war growth of southern cities brought immigrants, many from Latin America, along with "internal immigration" from other regions of the country. As Wright has shown, the most significant effects of this development were the disappearance of the low-wage economy and the growth of investment in land development, which promoted civic improvements and investment in education and infrastructure. Significant for understanding of Gaines' fiction, the pace of development has been greatest in Louisiana and Texas. A very large proportion of war-time spending went to the Gulf Southwest, where "more than half the total investment went into Texas, Louisiana, and Alabama, in that order" (Tindall 699-700,703).

As social historians have documented and as Gaines shows in his treatment of post-war black urban life, the effects of urbanization on blacks in the South were not entirely positive, especially in respect to unemployment and the family. As John Hope Franklin shows, "for many black newcomers to the city, employment failed to materialize. . .. Men were less likely to secure employment than women, thus replicating the Southern rural experience where the perception of black masculinity was constantly challenged at home and in the workplace"(421-22). Nonetheless, despite the enormous pressure of social change and continued prejudice, the black family remained relatively stable until about 1970. As Franklin states: "The sharp rise in black female-headed households since 1970 was the most significant indication of the deterioration of the black family" (422).

As a writer of fiction, Ernest Gaines has realistically described the effects of urbanization on southern black community. Discussion of Gaines' fiction has dealt frequently with two elements of his treatment of the transition to modernity: his representation of the black community and his stress on the black family. This critical approach has produced useful readings of the stories in *Bloodline*: for example, as Todd Duncan reads "Three Men," Procter Lewis is charged by an older male with the responsibility for changing his own relation to the black community. Todd Duncan writes: "Like the young college student [in "The Sky Is Gray"]. . . Procter is rebellious. The problem is that Procter's mind has been conditioned by an oppressive social situation and his energies confined to a circuit of peer-destruction which ultimately becomes self-destruction" (92). The origin of this self-destructiveness can be traced to the breakdown of family with the "deep sense of rejection" that he felt after the death of his mother, and there is no one in the family or community left to fill her role. Although he was on his way to becoming a habitual offender, a victimizer of his own community, Procter is saved by the paternal concern of Munford. As Duncan observes, the title of the story emphasizes "one of Gaines' most important concerns. . . the connection between generations and the acceptance of the responsibilities of literal or symbolic parenthood" (94).

Michel Fabre also centers his argument on the importance of a stable community: despite the increasing threat to order which mechanized agriculture poses, Gaines' "universe remains a stable one" (113). Fabre discovers a connection between the rural culture "where words are weighed" and a prose of "careful transcription by one who simply takes his time." Stressing the patient use of repetition and "brief passages where meaning fills the gaps," Fabre believes that a "waiting tension" which "explodes into tragedy" is characteristic of the Gainesian style.

The readings of Duncan and Fabre, along with the insightful criticism of Charles H. Rowell in "The Quarters: Ernest Gaines and the Sense of Place," view Gaines as an author recording "a static world fiercely resistant to change" (735). Accordingly, these critics have treated Gaines as a writer whose prose aesthetic reflects the qualities of rural life. Certainly this analysis identifies one aspect of Gaines' aesthetic, yet increasingly, especially in his more recent fiction but also in passages in the early stories, Gaines explores the consciousness of those who are alienated from the rural community. Even within the same work, the laconic, impassive naturalism which Fabre identifies as "Gainesian" may suddenly shift into a hurried, discontinuous, expressionistic style.

In *Catherine Carmier*, for example, the oppressive "circling" style of the passage in which Aunt Charlotte questions Jackson about his loss of faith is followed closely by the scene in which Jackson walks the field, hardly recognizing it as the place where he grew up. As the Quarters are destroyed by the encroachment of machinery, the emptiness of the land, its essential lack of meaning for Jackson, is mirrored in Gaines' style with its terse, direct sentences as mechanical in sound as the landscape has itself become. Not only have the old houses been torn down, but the trees have been cut and the wild blackberry and pecan patches have been plowed under. Without intrusive commentary, Gaines' style is allowed to speak of the emotional loss.

When dealing with the subject of technology, the mechanized farming which has destroyed Jackson's home place, the prose becomes purposeful, analytical, and transparent, suggesting the "classical" influence of Turgenev on Gaines' treatment of landscape. Yet this scene is followed almost immediately by Jackson's meeting with Catherine: the style now becomes fragmented, excited by broken phrases and rapid monosyllables. If Jackson was unable to identify with Aunt Charlotte's religious faith, he is also separated from Catherine, whose meaning he attempts to read "behind" her ordinary words and facial expression. She "seems" to be saying: "'All right, nothing can come of our love, but we can like each other, can't we? They can keep us apart, but they can't make us stop liking each other, can they?'" (125).

The richness and variety of this style derives from his attention to the specific situation and character. Indeed, Gaines' prose may be far more complex and varied than the author himself admitted when he spoke of "writing as well as I can," that is "writing cleanly, clearly, truthfully, and making it simple enough so that anyone might be able to pick it up and read it" (Rowell, "Interview" 49). Everywhere, passages in his work achieve nuances of style which reproduce the essential features of the subject. The frequency with which this subject is transition, not the static but the changing landscape of the South, produces an aesthetic capable of representing fragmentation, bewilderment, and despair.

Even in *Bloodline*, where stories such as "The Sky Is Gray" appear to record the pre-industrial culture, a harsh but loving community with its lessons of manhood and its rewards of identity and social acceptance, Gaines injects an inevitable "future" of modernity in which, albeit in his role as provider for his mother, James intends "next summer" to begin earning money by entering the larger economy as an agricultural worker. The town of Bayonne, a "little

bitty town" with "the pavement all cracked" and "grass shooting right
out the sidewalk," still manages to mark a transition from rural to
urban setting, for the lesson of racial division is enforced just as well
in Bayonne as in Baton Rouge. If James' visit to the dentist
represents the solace which he hopes to find "in town"and in the
future of accomplishment which he dreams of in the world beyond
Bayonne, the town is also peopled with enough prejudice and
indifference to challenge the child's future development. Danger
comes not just in the guise of a pimp who approaches his mother in
a cafe, but also in the divisive scene where a black student,
politicized and questioning the existence of God, argues against the
conventional beliefs of an elderly black preacher. As often, Gaines
seems skeptical of the contribution of the black church, which, as one
historian suggests, "operated largely in a context of fundamentalism
that excluded the social and economic issues of the day" (Tindall
566). Instinctively, James feels that he wants to emulate the student,
yet the student's questioning of tradition and of the meaning of
common language angers the listeners in the waiting room and
puzzles James. Significantly, perhaps, we never learn the reaction of
James' mother, Octavia, for James' attention is focused on the
college student, who quite possibly prophesies James' future faith: "'if
not in your God, then in something else, something definitely that
they can lean on'" (*Bloodline* 102).

On their way out of this underworld of the town, Octavia and
James are befriended by an elderly white couple, Helena and Alnest,
an ancient Sicilian couple whose grocery represents the old order of
human relations based on community rather than the individualistic
modern order of commerce. The "sale" of a quarter's worth of salt
pork turns out to be a gift rather than a commercial transaction,
until Octavia insists on fair payment, asserting her own worth and
providing a lesson for James. In this respect, the story confirms the
finding of social historians who conclude that traditionally the
number of blacks on public assistance was proportionately much
smaller among rural than urban populations (Tindall 547). In other
ways, traditional values seem to temper the ending of this story about

a youth's first awareness of urban life: the grocery is both home and business; Alnest, who is never seen, is ill and perhaps dying, but his and Helena's humanity is passed onto the child; James himself is thinking of the comfort of home, although the story implies that his character will be tested in the city, perhaps in Baton Rouge which looms in his memory as a place he once visited with his father.

In the story "Three Men" the setting shifts to the modern city, presumably Baton Rouge, although the scene could be any city jail. "Seven Spots," the tavern where Procter murders another black in self-defense, also ties the story to the urban setting. It is a roadside tavern which men visit in automobiles, where there is jukebox music and dancing, and where sexual encounters are easily arranged. It is also the locale where, as Munford eventually forces Procter to admit, blacks are perpetuating a cycle of violence against other blacks, and where the "brutish" treatment of women is part of the same cycle of defeated expectations. Gaines might almost be paraphrasing John Hope Franklin, who found that for the urbanized black male "unemployment and idleness brought on frustration, not infrequently culminating in abuse of family at home and criminal acts away from home"(422). Going to the penitentiary is one way for Procter to break the cycle, not as punishment but "'to sweat out all the crud you got in your system'" (141).

Munford presses Procter to consider, for the first time apparently, the question of his "manhood," his responsibilities as an adult within a larger community. Although the paradigmatic setting for an understanding of community and of generational responsibility may in fact be, as Charles H. Rowell states, the Quarters, the traditional lessons must be translated to the urban culture, for in the outline of modern history which Gaines implies, actual return to the rural culture is a frustrating and self-defeating gesture of nostalgia. More productive is what might be termed an imaginative return to history. Looking into history, as Jerry H. Bryant states, Gaines finds "that the enduring woman and the courageous man are the critical elements in the black race's existence and embody jointly, in their loving struggle of values, the characteristic features of life: change and growth. The political act, performed in courage, is the sign of growth, and implies both duration and satisfaction" (859).

In a temporary withdrawal from modernity, the Gainesian hero reviews his or her relation to rural traditions but does not plan to return to an actual agrarian life. Indeed, to a greater extent than has been realized Gaines' fiction implies an acceptance of, even an insistence on, change. Although Gaines describes rural life with nostalgia, he is well aware of the demographic shift of black population to the cities. Population figures show that in the South as a whole, the number of black farm operators declined from over 550,000 in 1950 to just over 85,000 in 1969. These numbers are mirrored in the statistics for Louisiana, where the 40,600 operators of 1950 declined to about 5,500 in 1969 (Smythe 291). Gaines' stories set in rural Louisiana reflect this black migration to the cities, where by 1980 eighty-one percent lived (Franklin 420).

Despite this reality Gaines is determined to preserve the cultural ties between urban present and rural past, particularly in terms of an ethos of family and community responsibility. In his treatment of the New South, Gaines suggests the need to draw on the past for ethical direction and the need to maintain a sense of one's ancestors as contributors to an evolving civilization. As William L. Andrews writes, Gaines explores an "understanding of progress as a conserving process." Andrews notes that Jane Pittman's story shows that "the folk has assumed over the years an identity based on progressive struggle, not socio-political struggle, but the struggle to recognize and conserve its spiritual resources and heroic folk traditions" (149).

Such an understanding of the past is implied in Todd Duncan's description of Mme Toussaint, the conjure woman in "A Long Day in November," who advises Eddie to burn his car if he wishes to regain his wife. Her wisdom derives from "a connection with intuition and to dimly remembered traditions on the Mother Continent" yet she is "testing Eddie's persistence and his readiness for change" (*Bloodline* 87). What Mme. Toussaint advises is not the return to an agrarian economy (since the story hints that Eddie may own an automobile again in the future) but she is suggesting a renewal of familial and communal relationships, which do not depend on an actual return to the rural way of life. Indeed, as Mme. Bayonne clearly sees in Catherine Carmier, the Cajuns have destroyed the Quarters forever by their land purchases and mechanized farming The remaining residents are permitted to live in the Quarters "as long as you keep your nose clean" (78), but for the young there is no alternative to urban migration. Nor does Gaines romanticize the agrarian way of life, for one sees everywhere in his stories examples of poverty and hardship among those who remain on the farm.

Gaines is also quite realistic in representing the demographic shift to the cities. The portrait of emigration from the Quarters that one reads in *Catherine Carmier* is confirmed by historical evidence, for by 1940 forty percent of southern blacks were town or city dwellers, and those who remained on farms found their position deteriorating, even in respect to jobs traditionally open to them (Tindall 570).

Gaines' narrative presents realistically the declining condition of farm life. Wideman has noticed the realism in *Of Love and Dust*, in which "Bonbon on his horse trailing Marcus is, among other things, a statement about the monotony and brutality of field labor" (80). Gaines certainly implies that much has been lost with the destruction of the Quarters and of similar rural communities, but the loss is irrevocable. The more important question is, given an understanding of the past, whether one will adapt to a future in an urban and industrial society. While the rural community providing a sense of human closeness and identity, it also involved hardships both physical and cultural, and these hardships increased with the encroachment of machinery on the tenant system. Not only did the mechanization of farm labor drive black workers from the land by reducing the demand for labor and by destroying the profitability of marginal land, it also reduced the standard of living for those who chose to remain on the farms. As Mabel Smythe writes, "The changes in methods and location of cotton cultivation, combined with the poverty of most black farmers, worked both to push Negroes out of farming and to make the attractions of city life irresistible" (288). The thesis that machines have taken jobs from rural blacks may be correct, but this does not lead Gaines to the conclusion that blacks should destroy "Western Civilization" and return to a pre-technological agrarian society, as the young radical, Billy, urges in *In My Father's House* (162). As a matter of fact, the more attractive characters in the fiction are not always rural survivors; role models appear equally often in urban settings, and may be connected with machinery and technology. As Alvin Aubert points out, in *Of Love and Dust* the character of "Jim Kelly, the plantation tractor driver and maintenance man. . . serves as a constant reminder to his ward, the intractable youth Marcus, of his responsibility for his own predicament" (72). Significantly, Jim Kelly finds his facility with machinery an asset, both in terms of making a living and fitting into the new social order. Because of his knowledge of machinery, he is able to talk easily with the cajuns and to earn the respect of whites and blacks.

As Rowell terms it, "the quarters in Gaines' fiction is a ritual ground of communion and community," a past to which Gaines must return in order to understand the present ("Quarters" 750). *Catherine Carmier* does not imply a continuing agrarian life for the young, but it does reach a hopeful resolution as the young re-enact through ritual the lessons of their ancestors. In fact, Mme. Bayonne assumes all along that Jackson will return to California after he has told his great-aunt of his plans, but the very act of telling her of his intention, what will amount to "'the worst moment of her life'" (70-71), may serve as a rite of passage through which Jackson will be enabled to transfer her essential lessons of humanity to an urban setting.

Perhaps the most significant treatment of modernity in Gaines' fiction is the novel *In My Father's House*. Set in the town of St. Adrienne, a growing community within commuting distance of Baton Rouge, the novel describes a locale which is in transition from rural to urban. Accompanying this social change, the major characters in the novel are defined according to their attitudes toward regional progress. The optimism of Rev. Philip Martin, the protagonist, is based on the belief that black southerners will achieve full economic participation in the New South's prosperity. During the post-war era St. Etienne has undergone a degree of racial progress, but after the death of Martin Luther King the civil rights movement faces challenges from outside, in the form of cajuns like Mr. Chenal, and from inside, as the black organization in St. Etienne has become stagnant and less solidified.

Even before the traumatic appearance of his son, Rev. Martin projects a sense of inertia and complacency. As his supporters notice a growing timidity and acceptance of gradualism, younger workers are impatient and seem merely to tolerate their leader on the basis of past accomplishment. The sense that Martin has lost enthusiasm for his public role is related to the fact that his belief in progress is a limited and materialistic answer to more complicated problems of modernization. Gaines suggests that Martin's complacency toward his role in social justice is reflected as well in a willingness to accept the "boosterism" of the town's white leaders, and that his weak grasp of both problems has its source in a failure of nerve. The inability to connect with others, an insistence on proud isolation, may be seen as Martin's psychological defense against society's ongoing attempt to degrade him.

As Gaines makes clear in an interview with Charles H. Rowell, the performance of the black father is conditioned by his position in society outside the home. As Gaines states, "I don't know that the father will ever be in a position. . . from which he can reach out and bring his son back to him again" (40). Martin also interprets his failure as a parent in the light of black history, excusing the abandonment of his first family as the result of a "paralysis" residue of slavery.

Part of the complexity of Gaines' treatment of character is illustrated in the way that Martin becomes a fully "rounded" character: his actions are understandable in human terms as the struggle for self-preservation of a proud, strong man, but from another point of view, they are rationalizations based on historical grounds. As his son, Robert X, implies, Martin's justification has come to seem weak rationalization, at least from the melancholy perspective of his son.

By the end of the novel, faced with the consequences of his

disregard of others (his son's suicide and the alienation of his second wife and children) Martin gives up, at least for the moment, his role as a community leader and questions his vision of the New South as a truly progressive coalition of blacks and whites. Gaines suggests no alternative to the spread of "progress" that has left Martin disaffected from those closest to him. However, Gaines insists on a critical examination, a tallying up, of the actual benefits and costs of development. At the heart of this examination is the fact that Martin's rise in fortunes operates as a defensive avoidance of the more strenuous task of maintaining a coherent identity in relation to family, community, and state. Martin's social position and wealth offer an illusory confirmation of self that leads him to lose sight of his own and others' human needs; his success masks his alienation from every form of intimacy.

In many ways Martin has endorsed the program of regional development promoted by white leaders in the South, and he has accepted a filter-down theory of economic reform. Though Martin "fights" the remaining businesses which discriminate, he only fights when he has the support of paternalistic white moderates, thereby collaborating with the town's white leadership by never pushing too hard. Surrounded by a group of whites and aging blacks as advisers, he speaks of waiting for the proper time for action and finding the proper means of protest. Having won privilege for himself, Martin epitomizes the historical problem of a separation of leadership from constituency within the civil rights movement (Tindall 568). Ironically, Martin may be more respected by whites, who envy his material prosperity and political power, than by blacks, who are able to see through the rhetoric of change to his underlying self-interestedness. Gaines' description of his residence as "the most expensive and elegant owned by a black family in St. Adrienne" (28) suggests Martin's relationship to the black community, for the expense and elegance of his home project his separation and defensiveness. His display of wealth is intended to cover an underlying insecurity which extends to every human relationship, most importantly that with his family. Epitomizing the New South ethos of success, Martin occupies a position of comfortable prominence, living in a large modern house and driving a luxury automobile. His expensive clothes are intended to impress others with his status, and he has come to believe that comfort and status are the ends of existence.

Certainly Martin wants these benefits for others, but by the same token he holds an exclusive position as long as they have not been extended to all. Howard Mills' accusation that his friend went "behind the backs" of his family and community in making a decision about calling off the boycott is the crux of Gaines' critique of the New South ethos. The modern South is morally corrupt, not because it has become industrialized and urbanized but because its pursuit of success has displaced the shared human values of communal life, including the practices of family and community involvement indecision-making. Even his closest supporter recognizes that Martin has failed to respect the rights of others, and especially the political right to choice. Countering Martin's statement that he acted for the benefit of his son in calling off the boycott, Mills says, "'We want this world better fit for everybody children. . . Not just for one man'"(127). That Martin has the potential for becoming an autocratic leader is suggested by the hints of past violence toward his own people, for we learn that in his youth the minister was twice picked up as a suspect in killings and for fighting (85).

There is also the carnal side to the Faust-like Martin, who tends to accept pleasure as his due and in return for political complacency: he has had many mistresses, enjoys rich food and drink, and his body has become soft and heavy. His striving after comfort and status characterize Martin as a representative of a certain New South boosterism, which Gaines undoubtedly intends to bring into question. Another point that connects Martin with the modern South is the facile way in which he claims to have "found God" (100). The re-appearance of Etienne, the alienated son from his first marriage, and Martin's effort to save him are events that completely upset his complacency. Martin is forced to admit the self-interest which underlies his faith in regional progress.

One aesthetic device appropriate to Gaines' interest in social reality is the use of setting to comment on a character's assertions. This realist technique is used in the passage which describes Martin's visit to Baton Rouge in search of Chippo Simon. Everywhere he looks in Baton Rouge, the setting refutes Martin's complacent faith in regional progress. Martin arrives on the same day that a young Vietnam veteran has been shot for stealing food, but we learn that similar acts of violence occur daily. At the heart of this underworld is East Boulevard, a street that Martin remembers as lively and prosperous, although even as he remembers it, East Boulevard was "a dangerous place" where "you could easily get yourself killed"(140). The district now shows the typical signs of urban blight: dilapidation, abandonment, darkness. While Martin does not yet see the connection between his "personal" life and the problems of the larger community, the ironic contrasts between his suburban lifestyle and the inner-city poverty of East Boulevard make the point clear. For example, the presence of Martin's automobile, which draws comment from nearly everyone he meets, is ironically contrasted with the setting in which most residents are on foot, exposed to the cold and rain. In this urban setting Martin feels even more isolated from people than in St. Etienne: he notices that he recognizes almost no one in Baton Rouge, the city where he apparently spent much of his youth, and with his narrow interest only in his own family, he has nothing in common with the individuals whom he meets.

The scene which describes Martin's first "conversation" with his son, Robert X (as he prefers to be called), reveals their differing views of existence. Ironically Martin attempts to make conversation by pointing out that spillways have brought progress to the area, a point of regional pride which elicits only silence and scorn on the part of his son. Martin speaks only of the future, predicting economic development which will presumably include blacks, but his future-orientation obviously masks a fear of examining the past and present. Turning his back on his son even as he attempts to re-connect with him, Martin adopts the same approach to Robert X as he has shown toward his current wife Alma and their children. He provides them with a comfortable life but, because of a history of guilt and insecurity, he holds himself apart. The origin of Martin's alienation, as his wife Alma analyzes it, is that he is trying to make up for the past. He has been "running" and has isolated himself (136).

When Martin offers the "excuse" that he had abandoned Robert's mother because he had been paralyzed by the pattern of slavery, he may have hit on the truth but he fails to see that his paralysis has not been alleviated by his participation in regional prosperity. His son rejects this argument entirely and judges his father without taking into account the impact of social conditioning on his father, yet the son is equally the product of this conditioning. His nihilism, his idea that "no matter what you do. . . they catch you off guard one day and break you"(27), arises from a personal history of defeat. Although the two men analyze the past in different ways (Robert X calls his father a "rapist" and labels his love "lust," while Martin asserts that he loved Robert's mother), both are perhaps partially correct: one can "love," in Martin's sense, and at the same time "rape," in Robert's sense. Ironically, both are partially justified, but neither can communicate his partial vision to the other.

In My Father's House represents a development of Gaines' style toward "a severe detachment, a distance between story and narrator," as Frank Shelton notes (340). As Gaines tells the story, he uses many fictional techniques to comment on his central character. Not only does Martin's perception of the setting clash with what is really there, what Martin says about the New South often conflicts with what he thinks. Through the omniscient narrator we enter a consciousness filled with self-doubt and evasion, a mind seduced by the material rewards of participation in progress but already doubting that these rewards are worth the price of personal isolation.

In several ways the novel's language is used to comment ironically on Martin's belief in progress. The description of his visit to the Quarters on Reno plantation includes a complex use of irony to distinguish between Martin's judgement about the "backwardness" of conditions there and the actual state of things: the emotional support and communal solidarity that makes a rich life possible even under difficult financial strain. Commenting on the narrative distance necessary to present Philip Martin, Gaines noted that the omniscient point of view was dictated by his character's isolation: "You cannot tell that story from the minister's point of view because the minister keeps too much inside him. . . he won't reveal it to anybody" (Rowell, "Interview" 41).

Although the treatment of Martin is often ironic, and particularly so when dealing with him as a representative of New South values, the irony is never so strong as to destroy the reader's sympathy for Martin. While we may suspect that his "paralysis" is partially the result of cowardice, we are also presented with a figure of considerable moral stature and emotional power. Ultimately, Martin rises above the level of pathos, a figure who elicits the reader's pity, to the level of tragedy, for through his character Gaines raises serious ethical issues and shows the destructive conflicts within a noble man attempting to meet conflicting responsibilities. Under the pressure of this conflict, he becomes tyrannical and blind, but finally realizes his condition. The character is successful because of Gaines' fidelity to a realistic aesthetic that places the character within a specific social setting, in this case the moment of the post-war South when the rising level of material prosperity, never extended fully to blacks to begin with, has collided against the psychological and emotional needs for a sense of the continuity of family and community.

Gaines' sense of assurance in pointing to ethical resolutions contrasts with the fragmentation and ambivalence of modernist writers in dealing with a similar landscape of social change. For Gaines, as for O'Connor, the machine connotes neither the ultimate destructiveness nor the seductive attraction that it suggested for Faulkner or Wright. His touchstone is always the actual quality of life within the social community. This perspective neither lauds technology as panacea nor dismisses its potential benefits, but the sober realism of his treatment insists on examining the actual consequences of change, much as O'Connor's comic realism unflinchingly records the material and psychological transformation of the post-war South.

Indeed, both Gaines and O'Connor depict the New South as a spiritual wasteland in which both individual identity and communal ties have been distorted by materialism and mechanization, yet neither finds a "solution" in fleeing the devastation. Rather, both writers suggest a re-consideration of the essential needs of human beings, including social and psychological needs that are largely unchanged by the transition from rural to urban life. The extent to which these needs are being met is a measure of the actual quality of life, not the mere quantity of change.

A similarity also exists between the use of the machine as symbol in the two writers: repeatedly the protagonist of a story must give up dependence on machinery in order to gain the wisdom to control it. As in the conclusions of O'Connor's *Wise Blood* and "The Life You Save May Be Your Own," in which the transforming moment of recognition arrives only after the protagonists give up or are defeated by the automobiles they prize, similarly Gaines suggests repeatedly that the power of machines and possessions conflicts with communal values in that ownership separates the individual from the social group and focuses one's labor on self rather than social needs. Both writers hold out the possibility of a sort of "redemption" of the mechanical realm, and by implication of the New South itself, but only after a new affirmation of the priority of human needs over mechanical technique. As Amy declares at the conclusion of "A Long Day in November," the family can anticipate owning an automobile again "'when you learn how to act with one'" (*Bloodline* 77). The increasing urbanization of the South threatens the black community, but as an external "environmental" force the threat can be dealt with by means of education that may take the form of knowledge passed down from elders or may as often involve difficult lessons learned by the young. Gaines urges his reader to consider the relationship of present to past, and to ponder the continuing existence of ethical choices of individual and political sorts whereby the impact of mechanization will be humanized. One should add that in the case of O'Connor, the modern devastation is more fundamentally a reflection of human nature itself, which in her view has always been largely mechanical and inhumane. Her fiction thus implies a less attractive notion of what human beings might be like in communal and traditional settings, such as Gaines' "Quarters."

One might profitably compare Ernest Gaines' treatment of modernization with that of another contemporary, William Styron. While Styron describes the transformation of war-time Norfolk, his home region and the home of many of his protagonists, nowhere does he provide the graphic evidence of change that one might expect, particularly when one considers that during the war Norfolk "achieved an unequaled reputation for squalor" (Tindall 702-3). Styron's reaction to the urbanization of the South is "aesthetic," based on the assumption of the writer's power to transform physical reality with an art that will replace the "monstrousness" of modern life with a serenity analogous to the effect of classical music. In comparison with this deliberately less realistic treatment of change and its social consequences, Gaines writes a more direct, realistic account of black neighborhoods in Baton Rouge in the sixties and seventies, as black businesses close, housing conditions deteriorate, and lives unravel.

In the fiction of Ernest Gaines, as in that of O'Connor and Styron, the New South after the Second World War is a subject which informs the aesthetic practice of the novelist in significant ways. To some extent Gaines' style, his use of point of view, his handling of comic and tragic genres, and his shaping of metaphor and symbolism is determined by an intention to record and change contemporary experience. With the eye of a powerful realist, Gaines has carefully set down his vision of the post-war South. With the development of his work from *Bloodline* through *In My Father's House*, Gaines has shown an ability to adapt his realist aesthetic to the demands of the imaginative subject in ways that we are only beginning to appreciate.

Chapter 10

Walker Percy's Critique of Technology

As I have shown in tracing Allen Tate's dialogue with the Victorian
aesthetic of Arnold and Ruskin, modern southern writers continued
the nineteenth-century debate over the relationship of art to science.
Often, the Victorian view of science involved an abnegation of the
secular world of science and commerce, while the artist claimed
authority over the spiritual and aesthetic realms. At the end of the
century William Morris "considered poetry a means of calling up a
beauty vanished from a mechanized world." Like many writers of his
generation he expressed the fear "that as mechanization expands the
affective life declines" (Sussman 4). Opposing a romantic organicism
to the rational mechanistic philosophy that dominated a strand of
Victorian thinking, Morris and others promoted a society which
returned to hand-labor and crafts as a means of escaping the
corrupting influence of technology. Raymond Williams has asserted
that for John Ruskin "industrial society is necessarily bad--and art
impossible in it." In line with this late-Victorian reaction many
twentieth-century modernists stress the negative potential of science
and technology. Carlyle's warning of "the submergence of the
individual in the organization, the dependence on 'machinery' rather
than the self" (Sussman 20) is echoed in writers such as Hemingway,
O'Neill, Pound, Eliot, and Yeats, and continues to be heard today
from neo-agrarian southerners. For many modernists the retreat from
science and technology led in the direction of new sources of
spiritual authority. Eliot's doubts about the validity of modern

civilization result in his search for a "united religion-- [a] social code of behavior that repeats Carlyle in certain respects"(Williams 34).

In southern literature the reaction against technology surfaces as a major concern during the late nineteenth century. Whether critical of the machine, as in the reaction of Sidney Lanier, or promoting the New South's rapid industrialization, the position adopted by the majority of regional writers, southern writers of the time accepted the assumption that the machine radically affected the private life and the social community. This assumption, though treated in quite different ways, was shared by the southern writers of the twenties and thirties. Because of the South's rural character and its social traditionalism, one would expect a dismissal of industrialism among its best writers, and in the post-war generation of the Nashville Agrarians this to some extent is certainly the case.

Following the Second World War, however, southern writers began to look upon industrialization with a new realism. The impulse toward the technological sublime, the sense of mystery and power associated with machinery in the late nineteenth century, does not manifest itself as strongly, not even on the consciousness of Flannery O'Connor's apparent *naifs* (who are never as naive as they seem to be). In writers such as O'Connor and Ernest Gaines, the southern literary response to technology contributed to a humanistic reappraisal of the nature of technological society. Although the modernists of the twenties and thirties had depicted technology as a wasteland, the interrelationship of art and technology in the writing of the fifties and sixties becomes considerably more complex, reflecting more pluralistic responses. The modernist persuasion that technology was directly responsible for, or at least the means of, an ongoing destruction of environment and an undermining of the sense of human community is challenged if not refuted.

Not all southern writers of the post-war generation, however, participated in this more realistic appraisal of technology. Walker Percy returned the southern treatment of industrialism to many of the assumptions of the Agrarians, who attacked the negative effects of industrialism on the South while not always insisting on a literal return to agrarian practices. Percy's insistence that he is writing as a post-modern, as one who looks beyond the "old Auto Age" into the age of appropriate technology, masks the fact that many of his criticisms of science repeat familiar apocalyptic visions of the technological sublime, positions that Tate and even Faulkner had begun to work through. Walker Percy's "post-modern" scenario is surprisingly Victorian in its prudishness and its nostalgia for a cohesive form of belief. Like many Victorians, Percy speaks of scientific rationalism as destructive of the spiritual and artistic life; he also points toward an inevitable apocalypse in which the "old" science will be replaced by "genuine" science, one which will make room for organic, dynamic, and transcendent aspects of experience. As we shall see, this "genuine" science consists of a return to Christian belief in that Percy wants science to "expand" its empirical method to admit new "facts" of manifestations of the supernatural.

The new technology envisioned by Percy prioritizes environmental and quality-of-life concerns. Meanwhile, the problems of "old" technology are largely ignored: how to deal with displaced workers of the industrial belt, what to do with ravaged cities and how to clean up polluted sites are matters that enter the fiction only as evidence of the apocalypse underway in those segments of society that the new age has not touched. For the more fortunate inhabitants of Percy's suburban South, the new age replaces industrial production, not with Morris' craft culture, but with a service society populated with white-collar professionals engaged in information, medical, and leisure occupations.

As a result the endings of Percy's novels often leave the protagonists isolated, living on cultural islands where the problems of the old technology cannot intrude. These idealistic conclusions show us constructive applications of appropriate technology, controlled and directed by human beings whose lives are focused on the private issues of spiritual integration and quality-of-life, but the novels fail to explain what has happened to the remainder of society, nor do they explain how such "old" technologies as basic urban services continue to function. Also, by limiting the description of labor to the professional class, Percy rather optimistically suggests that the traditional problems of labor such as the accomplishment of good wages and favorable working conditions have altogether disappeared. To an even greater extent than the conservative Agrarians, Percy describes a world which enjoys the benefits of technology and the comforts of modern life, while at the same time he disclaims responsibility for industrial and service workers who make quality of life possible in the suburbs.

The most serious criticism of technology in Walker Percy's writing concerns its having replaced the spiritual quest as the focus of modern life. As Glenn H. Utter concludes, "Walker Percy himself does view science and technology as a threat to human beings, but this threat originates in man's willingness to make his machines and techniques the governing center of his life" (125). In this respect, Percy's disdain for social psychology, especially the contemporary effort to arrive at self-knowledge from an endless analysis of sexual feelings, permeates *Lost in the Cosmos: The Last Self-Help Book*, a book which parodies the mechanical approach of many self-help texts as well as the uncritical acceptance of such books by the mass reading audience. In a final section of the same book Percy satirizes a "survival mission" to another planet planned by Aristarchus Jones, whose first acts include "group therapy sessions in self-knowledge." Derisively he describes the futuristic colony, which adopts the principles of B. F. Skinner's *Walden Two* "modified by Jungian self-analysis" in offering a double-edged behavior modification program designed to silence dissent and quash "eccentric" views, including religious or "mystical" ideas.

The character of Aristarchus Jones is satirized not because his temperament is scientific rather than humanistic, but because he applies a simplistic model of science to complex human behavior. As Percy insists repeatedly in his non-fictional writing on language, the linguistic behavior of human beings, the unique ability for self-consciousness and for the assertion of selfhood, necessitates a more complex study of human nature than natural or social science has yet undertaken. Jones's behaviorism reduces the complexity of language to the level of stimulus-response, while his apparently enlightened group therapy takes on the brutal coerciveness of totalitarian systems if we recall that "exile" from the community of the planet Europa amounts to extinction. There is an aesthetic as well as an ethical basis to Percy's disdain of popular psychology. The author of *Lost in the Cosmos* seems to reject sexual self-help manuals with the same distaste which characterizes Sutter's disapproval of *The Art of Loving*, Rita Vaught's much prized self-help volume. It is, in part, simply a matter of old-fashioned "manners": as Sutter remarks, "I never really approved your using technical terms like 'penis envy' in ordinary conversation" (*The Last Gentleman* 246).

Lost in the Cosmos continues Percy's central concerns about technological society. Picking up where the essays of *The Message in the Bottle* left off, the later essays focus on the limitations of semiology and deconstruction rather than on behaviorism and structuralism. Semiotics, Percy suggests, is based on a theory of language which is reductionist in its depiction of communication as a quantity of signs exchanged between communicators. It fails to account for the mystery underlying the denotative function of language, the fact that every use of the verb "to be" implies a triadic relation among object, perceiver, and a transcendent consciousness.

Because these concerns with linguistics are by no means limited to his non-fiction, Percy's essays illuminate a reading of his fiction. In *Lost in the Cosmos* (the title echoes the popular public television series hosted by Carl Sagan, to which Percy refers in a footnote on pages 201-202), Percy sketches a lengthy scenario by which the competing interests of science and the humanities are integrated. The twentieth-century acceleration in the pursuit of scientific knowledge, accompanied by the neglect of spiritual study, will ultimately lead to the realization of the limits of science and technology, a limitation which the true scientist willingly admits. The very expansion of empirical science will lead to an alienation of crisis proportions. Ultimately, the only solution to the "predicament" brought about by science, the growing sense of abstraction and alienation from ourselves, is the "preposterous remedy" of a return to

Judaeo-Christian faith" (*Lost in the Cosmos* 254).

Percy is restating a point he had made in "Culture: the Antimony of the Scientific Method" where he called for "a more radically scientific method" which recognizes "that there is a metascientific, metacultural reality." The apocalypse, the very rupture which has thrust the modern into the post-modern age, is the direct result of the emphasis on "traditional" science and technology (that is, science based on dyadic or empirical method as opposed to the "new" science based on an understanding of "triadic" relationships implicit in the problem of language and existence itself), and especially may be traced to the compulsion to replace spiritual learning with technical knowledge, or as Jacques Ellul would see it, the necessity for technique to extend to all areas of human life, replacing human freedom with a technical model of efficiency.

As one would expect, Sutter Vaught, the brilliant diagnostician, has understood the problem better than most, though it may also be true, as Barrett intuits, that Sutter's radical skepticism merely inverts Rita's abstraction from experience. Sutter's belief that lewdness is the "sole concrete metaphysic of the layman in an age of science" (*The Last Gentleman* 279) is echoed in a number of Percy's essays describing a "deranged age" along the same lines as Sutter's diagnosis. Will Barrett, as John Edward Hardy points out, finally rejects the modern age in which the pleasures of technology and, as Percy repeatedly phrases it, "genital" sex have displaced the traditionalist's understanding of the self.

As John Edward Hardy writes, "the entire lengthy narrative of the love affair and attendant misadventures. . . is important in the final analysis only as a record of the trials the hero must undergo in preparation for his ordeal in the desert" (61). It is not coincidental that industrialism was accompanied by the growth of pornography (*Lost in the Cosmos* 10), for pornography and abstract science, that is, the immanent and transcendent selves, are the "only" two alternatives remaining to the alienated modern (*Lost in the Cosmos* 122). Lancelot, Percy's most fully drawn pornographer and a character whom Percy has described as "insane," investigates every avenue of immanence, as he compares himself to pre-Einsteinian scientists seeking diligently but with the wrong assumptions. Like those earlier investigators, Lancelot's intelligence is unearthing repeated signals that his worldview is fundamentally wrong, yet he has no theory to account for the experimental data he is gathering. In Lancelot's case, in despair of finding an adequate theory, he slips into a self-absorbed life of sensation and pleasure. Nonetheless, in so far as he is radically alienated from conventional experience, Lancelot is no madman: he is entirely typical of Walker Percy's questing heroes.

Percy appropriates the example of Einstein to show a scientist dissatisfied with the limits of science, searching for an approach to truth beyond those available to conventional science. Lancelot's violent rejection of secular experience, however, goes well beyond Einstein's discovery of the limits of Newtonian science, for while both understand that science is an open-ended process of theorem and proof (a process whose priority Lancelot seeks to discredit) the analogy appears more than a little misleading. Lancelot's search for truth beyond science points toward a return to spiritual authority, while Einstein's political activity outside the laboratory pointed toward a humanist ethics.

Lancelot's apocalypse arrives with his own disillusionment in science and in marriage. Thus, with his wife Margot discovered in adultery, a "New World" opens up for Lancelot. It is similar to the childhood experience when he discovered his father's involvement in political graft, and like the earlier discovery, the knowledge that he is not the father of Siobhan is "not necessarily a bad thing" (*Lancelot* 42). Until the climactic event, the fiery destruction of Belle Isle along with Margot, her lover, and the Hollywood film crew, Lancelot is indeed the pornographer-technologist, the"engineer" whom Glenn Utter describes as "Ellul's technologist who, in trying to bring a mystery into the light of rational analysis, discovers that it has vanished"(123).

Though considerable ambiguity surrounds Lancelot's relationship to Percival, the priest-psychologist to whom he narrates his life's story, and to Anna, the rape victim with whom he fantastically hopes to begin a new life in "old" Virginia, the Percival and Lancelot relationship turns into a sort of meditation on the possibility of salvation from modernity, that period of history in which the fundamental problem is authentic communication, the ability to connect with others beyond the closed self. Whether Lancelot "solves" the problems of communication, whether he actually arrives at the understanding of himself necessary for communication, is never answered, but the novel does succeed in its depiction of the moment of despair and the moment of hope that follow immediately upon the collapse of faith in modernity. As we have seen earlier, it is a moment not unlike the despair of the early Allen Tate, with his dramatic "iron forestries of hell" in "The Subway," or Faulkner's disgust with the shoddiness of modern production accompanied by the embarrassing decline of morality. Percy's reaction against modernity, however, is even more resolute and passionate, and it points toward more radical solutions than those implied by Faulkner, Tate, or even O'Connor.

In the case of Sutter, for example, his destructive theories are the gauge of his personal despair, itself the result of his keen diagnosis of the problem of modern existence. The traditional language of ethical choice does not work, contemporary society, having suffered the loss of conviction in any language by which the triadic nature of human communication may understand itself. Science has developed to the point that it understands physical nature thoroughly, but the study of the self has failed to keep pace. The pleasure that Binx Bolling or Will Barrett, living in Kierkegaard's aesthetic sphere, takes in the particularity of the concrete world comforts a self that is radically uncertain of its own identity. Still, the aesthetic realm is only a temporary solution, merely a putting off of the decision that one must make if one is to live authentically. The choice is, of course, to live like Sutter in total immanence or to acknowledge transcendence as an eternal and omnipotent presence in human life.

In terms of language theory Percy describes the mistaken approach of behaviorists and semioticians as examples of attempts to deny the uniquely human element in consciousness. A parody of the behaviorist appears in *Love in the Ruins* in the figure of Art Immelman, the bureaucrat con-man who seizes on Dr. Tom More's invention, the lapsometer, as cure for the emotional disorders of modern man. The result is not only an outbreak of class warfare but, more thematically pertinent, a reduction of speech to a babel of tongues. The purely mechanical theory of language and human psychology eliminates inhibitions that had been preserved by the awareness of the special nature of language as symbolic experience. Still, Immelman's suggestion that all human difficulties can be" solved" by means of a technological advance in machinery is satirized in his very appearance: he reminds More of a sleazy used-car salesman in the "old" auto-age. Not only is his theory misguided, his technology is itself outdated. He is representative of the layman's naive conception of the application of science, the extravagant hope that science may bring about a utopia that the genuine scientist, better informed about science's limitations, is more hesitant to claim. As Percy writes in *Lost in the Cosmos* only the layman expects science to provide omniscience; the genuine scientist acknowledges "the meagerness of knowledge in his own field" and understands the narrow limits of scientific truth (119). The difficulty is that the layman, expecting science to serve as a panacea for human problems, is ignorant of the existence of the entire realm of spiritual problems for which science has no answers.

The climax of each of Percy's novels involves a critique of the effects of this naive faith in science and technology. The death of Lonnie in *The Moviegoer*, Lancelot's act of vengeance against his unfaithful wife and her lover, the re-establishment of communication between couples in *Love in the Ruins* and *The Second Coming* are examples of a focus on the language of technique. *The Thanatos Syndrome*, in which Dr. Tom More studies the reduction of modern language to contextless phrases, continues the critique of the decline of modern language as it is used by therapists and technicians.

Another important representation of the loss of communication is the scene in which Will Barrett attends Jamie's deathbed in *The Last*

Gentleman. Set in the New Mexican desert near the location where Oppenheimer, "luckiest of all abstract men," helped institute the atomic age, the scene examines the modern abstraction of the language of death and the effect of the application of "technique" to such private human spheres as the death of a friend or family member. With humorous irony Percy describes Barrett's troubled sense that Jamie was not "properly" sick. Though medical science was in fact unable to treat his condition or relieve his suffering, Barrett feels reflexively that a proper death in a technological age should be attended by the emblems of a technological society: that is, by machines, devices which heal or relieve suffering. Instead, Barrett finds Jamie attended by an apparently inept staff in a sparsely equipped clinic.

In addition to the "inconsequence and unprovidedness of Jamie's illness," Jamie is himself using a language of which Barrett is an inexperienced and faulty interpreter, as Jamie begins "hearing words according to some fashion of his own" (*The Last Gentleman* 370). The arrival of a local priest with the fatuous manner of an American League umpire again upsets the engineer's expectation that every human activity should have its appropriate technology: Barrett even expects the priest to carry a special "kit" for baptism and is shocked when he simply asks for a glass of tap water.

Percy envisages a "new age" following the apocalypse brought about by the entropic tendency of science itself. Characterized by the shift of society away from belief in technology, if not by the actual discarding of technological benefits, the new age will move away from reliance on technology and will admit that science does not contribute essentially to human understanding of the self. Despite his legal "insanity," one of Percy's finest diagnosticians for the new age is Lancelot, the prisoner who describes the life he will establish after release from the institution where he is held. As Lancelot insists, the past, in which a secure faith in conventional truths was possible, has been replaced by a "post-modern" age in which we "must begin all over again" (*Lancelot* 66). Although Lancelot possesses no idea of a solution, and he apparently has no future in "old Virginia," his diagnosis is clear and exact. Its similarity with similar analyses in Walker Percy's non-fiction indicates that it is the author's analysis as well.

In terms of its treatment of science and technology, and in other respects as well, this "absolutely new" future is not really new at all. Though the fictional treatment seems new, with its focus on futuristic technology, space exploration, and psychological "discoveries," the author's representation of modernity is in many respects familiar, recalling the Victorian and Agrarian sense of an apocalyptic crisis brought on by unmanageable technological change. Percy's "shock" at the assault of technology may be part of a broader cultural return that characterizes the post-sixties.

Furthermore, the nostalgia for traditional life in Percy's work, like the romanticizing of farming in the writings of Wendell Berry may be read as a rhetorical assertion, a complaint against the machine at the moment when the application of advanced electronic technology has become essential and when a genuine retreat from modernity is unthinkable. At this cultural moment, when technology is really beyond debate, it becomes appealing to suggest a return to craft culture, to small town "personal" existence, and to spiritual life and "values." In one sense this effort to return is the predictable nostalgia of an advanced society for simpler and more "meaningful" ways. In another sense, however, the historicizing of the pre-industrial past is an expression of the eighties' consciousness of its very own distance from the pre-technological past and from those traditional values that it speaks of recovering.

As Allen Tate noted, the Victorian response to the initial wave of industrialization was a fatalistic sense of powerlessness. In response late nineteenth-century writers such as John Ruskin tended to separate "art" from the contemporary world of business and practical affairs. Matthew Arnold's "abdication" of common reality resulted in a diminished subject for art, one symptom of which was the inability of modern writers to produce epic. Instead, to the extent that moderns focused solely on technique, it was not a sign that they were engaged in a meaningful critique of technology. Instead, the rise of craft and technique as aesthetic touchstones of art, an aesthetic movement that in America culminated in a mechanical approach to criticism focused on close reading (Ransom's suggestion that if he could not discover an ambiguity, he would create one) was for Tate proof of the artist's relegating control of art to science, thus admitting the inability of artists to make sense of physical nature. Further, genuine efforts to understand the past resulted in mere gestures of historicism, and those contemporaries who professed the most identification with the past, as did Eliot with his nostalgia for king, church, and country, had experienced most acutely the loss of historical connection. Historicism was the most telling symptom of the modern's abandonment of contemporary reality and of a truly historical imagination.

Walker Percy's critique of the contemporary South is a recounting of modern disaffection with urban-industrial life. Southern suburbs, however, are not depicted as the jungles of competition, aggression, and neurosis that Percy observes in urban centers. Modernity is diseased, but a peculiar dispensation extends to the southern suburbs, which take on the Dickensian quality of refuge from the workplace, a feminized home contrasting with the male urban world of labor and technology.

The special dispensation accorded the southern suburb is immediately apparent in Percy's last novel, *The Thanatos Syndrome.* The novel diagnoses a spiritual disorder which points to an apocalyptic devastation precipitated by secular faith in progress, while its protagonist, an aging and recently de-institutionalized Dr. Tom More, settles into the suburban lifestyle with the relaxed complacency of the "failed" but well-to-do professional. The optimism of More's youthful discovery of Freud, his belief that "people can get better, can come to themselves, without chemical and with a little help from you" (17), is parallelled by his admiration of "old style" southerners, who are shown to "get along" better than either liberals or "new" conservatives (36). Like the young Binx Bolling, and like many another protagonist in the novels, More makes a sufficient income from seeing a few clients at his home office, but barely enough to interrupt his sailing of paper airplanes at the martin house. The financial independence of Percy's characters has the appeal of escapism, understandable in an age of national economic decline. If need be, there is family money or connections to fall back on. Even the devastation of progress hasn't changed the fact that in the genteel South there always seems to be an uncle, cousin, or fraternity brother on whom one can call.

Walker Percy, we may conclude, envisages a period of corrupt modernity which must be replaced with a new age, a new start in science, art, and, most importantly, language itself. Nonetheless, this new age in many ways consists of a return to old ways: to spiritual study over science, to the professional class over industrial labor, and to social conservatism over social experiment. Paradoxically, while this new age views technology as inherently outdated, its inhabitants continue to enjoy the benefits of an advanced technological society and of the labor which it requires for production and distribution. As every novel from *The Moviegoer* to *The Thanatos Syndrome* implies with their loving descriptions of gadgetry (not unlike those of Ian Fleming on a more popular level) modern southerners remain fascinated with the diversions of modernity. However, as George Orwell noted in one of his periodical reviews, a modern work of literature that argues for "spirituality" as opposed to "materialism" is likely to be "a plea for the simple life, based on dividends. Rejection of the machine is, of course, always founded on tacit acceptance of the machine" (312).

Nonetheless, the rhetoric of the new age is tied to some very significant ideological positions. Responsibility for the realm of labor associated with industrial production is disavowed, while the problems of urban centers are dismissed because they are also symbolically of the "old" age. The new age is suburban, and for males the suburb's recreational centerpiece is the golf course. Consequently, the etiquette, landscape, and even the technique of the game appear fraught with symbolic meaning in Percy's fiction. While it may be populated with less than appealing types (the southern bigot, the complacent businessman, the hypocritical clergyman) the golfcourse is nonetheless the setting of much of the fiction, the locale for the apocalypse and the beginning of the new age, hide-out for unruly blacks arguing revolution and the place where one discovers oneself falling, a symptom of spiritual malaise.

Complementing these male golfers are females who are essentially domestic, the daughters of upper-middle-class families who support them until such time as they marry and are supported by their husbands. Those females who do work take on remarkably conventional "feminine" occupations, as does "nurse" Ellen even in her second career as real estate saleswoman. The rebelliousness of many other female characters is not a sign of their break with their class; rather, it is a gesture of social privilege that is understood, even to some extent expected, of young women as a form of "self-expression." As John Hardy has pointed out, actual labor is a subject that is largely missing from Percy's novels. It comes as something of a shock to realize how little detail appears in the descriptions of industrial or technological labor, and one discovers instead an idyllic suburb with neither the drudgery of an actual agrarian existence nor the harassment of urban life.

In *The Thanatos Syndrome* Dr. Tom More relates that, despite his objections to the intolerance and ignorance of some of his neighbors in Feliciana Parish, he would choose to live nowhere else. Located a decent but not inconvenient distance from New Orleans, the city on which it actually depends, this edenic retreat of affluence and benevolence fosters a cultural split-identity toward the machine and toward technology: dismissing technological development as either "old fashioned" (in the sense of the "old" Auto Age) or "unspiritual," the suburbanite continues to enjoy and even consciously to extoll the benefits of modernity.

Optimistic in their general outlook and conservative in their social views, suburban southerners do not admit many implications of recent technological change, such as the increasing stratification of social classes in America or the concentration of wealth in the professional class. The novels of Walker Percy portray the suburban South and its imaginative return to neo-Agrarian responses to technology. In the face of a changing South that is indeed post-modern, the protagonists in Walker Percy's novels tend to dismiss modernity rather than to see themselves as participants in the technological present.

Postscript

The direction of southern literature since the sixties has seemed to many readers to have abandoned a distinctively southern aesthetic and to have entered the mainstream of American literary culture. Younger authors who have emerged since 1970 including Harry Crews, Richard Ford, Josephine Humphreys, Bobbie Ann Mason, Toni Morrison, Anne Tyler, and Alice Walker, as well as older writers who continue to create new work, present for the most part a portrait of the South as a region not much different from the rest of the country. So much has the South changed, with the mushrooming of its cities and the industrialization of its work force, that Walker Percy has questioned whether distinctive regional differences any longer exist, and Walter Sullivan has proclaimed the death of the "southern novel."

However one may feel about the undeniable decline of the agrarian and traditional South, the literary culture of the New South continues many elements of the past. The fiction of Anne Tyler or Bobbie Ann Mason, though it is more likely to locate the southerner in a suburban community, is still focused on elements of belief and social life that are identifiably "southern." Contemporary examinations of the racial past in Alex Haley's *Roots* or Alice Walker's *The Color Purple* have produced some of the most significant literary work of the past decades. Peter Taylor's *A Summons to Memphis* continues the writer's delightfully sensitive re-creation of an earlier generation of genteel southerners, while the southern poor white of Harry Crews or Cormac McCarthy remain a distinctive literary genre.

Although no consensus exists in terms of these writers' attitudes toward mechanization, certain generalizations may be attempted. For a generation coming of age in the sixties, there is a tendency to move beyond the modernist fear and awe of technology toward efforts to control and humanize it. To some extent Flannery O'Connor was the precursor, writing with comic wit of changes that she felt were irreversible and, in a certain sense, irrelevant. The social and economic change that has become even more apparent since the sixties, with southerners beginning to speak of Atlanta as the region's metropolis and of Birmingham and Memphis as themselves "metropolitan," has opened similar possibilities for comic appreciation and social satire. The analysis of psychological pressures involved in the migration of southern families to the cities is a central feature of Anne Tyler's vision in novels such as *A Slipping-Down Life*, *Earthly Possessions*, and *Dinner at the Homesick Restaurant*. For Josephine Humphreys the instability of social relationships is the subject of two fine novels, *Dreams of Sleep* and *Rich in Love*.

Even those who, like Alice Walker, question technological progress in terms of its effects on the individual and the environment, are accustomed to, if not comfortable with, the existence of pervasive technology. In *Horses Make a Landscape More Beautiful*, a collection of poems with strong ecological and humanistic criticisms of technology, Walker is able to "see through" the machine and to view it as the mere agent of human decision-making. In fiction, essays, and poetry Walker has articulated her generation's concerns about the costs of technological development in environmental and human terms. Walker's satire is critical of suburban life as well as of modern dependence on automobiles and other machines. Walker valorizes, on the other hand, the image of the simple mechanic, the early or pre-industrial artisan, and she also shows the subsistence farmer as a symbolic image which connects economic independence and ecological concern.

It is of course the very notion that technology can be managed, that the machine is not the "iron demon" of Victorian writing, that marks the break between modernist and post-modernist visions of technology. Faulkner's tragic vision of the disappearing wilderness, the shrinking triangle of delta hunting land that Issac McCaslin revisits each year, is foreign to the experience of most contemporary southerners. The aesthetic shift may well be signaled by the fact that the southern writer now appears to feel alien in the rural landscape: the "country" has become a place to be visited or the object of nostalgic daydream, a "simpler past" of one's grandparents to which one returns only in dreams. In reality southern fiction is now largely urban, or suburban, in setting, and its aesthetic reflects a culture that may still think of itself as "southern" but that is determined in many respects by the general American culture. The fact is nowhere more pertinent than in relation to the complex work of Richard Ford, whose novel *The Sports-writer* and stories in *Rock Springs* are subtly ironical representations of the southern consciousness largely, though not entirely, dissociated from the basic elements of regional identity: the sense of history, family, and community.

The post-sixties generation in the South feels little real discomfort with technology itself. Indeed, like a new toy, the wealth and suburban lifestyle that have emerged throughout the region have perhaps been accepted more readily in the South than elsewhere. Despite seemingly obligatory bows toward the ancestral past, southern writers like Walker Percy have shaped a fiction that appears to accurately reflect the New South's acceptance of a corporate and professional ethos, albeit a professional ethos that senses its own want of spiritual direction. Others like Ernest Gaines have examined the human problems of transition to modernity and called into question the "progress" that the New South has brought, but Gaines has nonetheless accepted the fact of modernization as irreversible.

Few contemporaries, however, feel threatened by the force that Jacques Ellul found in a self-expanding "technique," the conception of the machine as organic and self-directing that can be traced from Victorian to modernist writing. Ellul's assumption that technique is an autonomous "organic" mechanism has been largely dismissed. However deleterious the ecological and psychological dangers of technology, the post-war generation seem convinced that technology can be directed by human choice. Alice Walker's critique, even with its fantasies of pre-industrial ways of life, assumes the opposite of Ellul's modernist analysis, for her populism implies that mechanization can be controlled and can serve humane goals.

Likewise, in other writers of the seventies and eighties the ambivalent mixture of glamour and destructiveness that urbanization invoked in Faulkner's generation (in the sojourn of southerners such as Wolfe and Tate in New York one felt the southern writer's sense of excitement as well as a David-like ambition of defeating the urban Goliath on his own turf) is replaced by an apathetic acknowledgement of urbanization, and by a new interest in more liveable secondary and provincial cities, and in small towns. The conventional motif of the rural southerner starting out for the big city has been reversed: now the urban southerner may well be headed, as Alice Walker appears often to be, for the personalism and authenticity of the small town or at least for a limited "community" within the city.

The attitudes toward modernization embedded in this return are not entirely obvious: unlike the commune movement of the sixties and early seventies, which usually implied a rejection of technology or a search for a simpler "appropriate" technology, the glamorization of small town and family in the eighties does not imply an actual rejection of the benefits of technology. The friendly white houses with their picket fences are now an intriguing facade, for behind them the homes are filled with electronic equipment and are linked to, indeed supported by, economic decisions toward the larger world made in the urban-industrial workplace or in the service industries that have replaced it, and that may be recreating in less obvious forms many of the social and personal pressures characteristic of industrialism. Those who retreat behind the white-picket fence, whether literally or imaginatively, embrace a surprisingly high-tech view of the outside world and continue to experience the ambivalence toward technological society that is reflected in southern fiction. The new Victorian cottages in America's suburbs come complete with double garages, and those garages are apt to conceal expensive imported automobiles that further link the new southerner to a national and world economy.

Indeed, the "fortressing" of the middle class in the eighties provides a significant subject for fiction and satire. The black middle class, with its discovery of the ethos of business and bourgeois consumption, is the subject of some of Ishmael Reed's most interesting work. In "Native Son Lives!" (from *Shrovetide in Old New Orleans*) Reed points out that the black middle class is concerned with crime and with misconceived welfare spending, while at the same time he asserts the black businessman as the social model, suggesting in "Image and Money" that "free enterprise is not a bad idea and has produced art" (53). In a "Self-Interview" Reed quotes architect Max Bond: "No one has been able to maintain an environment and improve it without money. Without means, without some sense of worth that comes from having a job, having money, being a productive element of the society" (164). While Reed grudgingly admits the need for some governmental supervision, such as the enforcement of antitrust laws on large corporations, his views are distinctly pro-business and pro-development. The radicalism of the past is dismissed as either irrelevant or misguided: "The sixties was a strident decade. I call it 'The Decade that Screamed.' It's going to take hard working critics to sift through all of this and separate the substance from the noise" (142).

Authors such as David Madden and Harry Crews write of a South that is more suburban and more mechanized than that of the earlier generations. Despite the continuing voice of critics such as Andrew Lytle and Walter Sullivan, both of whom have ties with the Agrarian movement at Vanderbilt, the perspective of most southern writers replicates national concerns. Increasingly southerners such as Richard Ford, Ernest Gaines, and Anne Tyler live and write outside the region and maintain sometimes tenuous connections with the South. This ambiguous relationship is evident in Ishmael Reed's mulling over his identity as a "southern" writer: "I left when I was four years old. . . I don't know much about the place. But I have a lot of it in me" (234). Nonetheless, Sullivan's warnings in *Death by Melancholy* that the loss of strong regional identity will lead necessarily to a decline of art have not been borne out, as evidenced by the many talented writers who have come of age in the seventies and eighties.

Nor has the sense of an aesthetic tradition been entirely lost. Although contemporaries such as Mason or Ford may not assert their ties with regional artistic tradition, they do continue to draw upon the conventions of southern fiction for many artistic effects. The motif of the rural outsider's entrance to the modern city, for instance, continues a staple of southern storytelling. In the work of Bobbie Ann Mason, David Madden, Harry Crews, and James Dickey, one preserves the sense of rural origins and ties of southerners who have become urbanized only within the last generation. A particularly interesting example of a writer examining the recent arrivals in the modern culture is Lee Smith, a talented and sophisticated storyteller who draws heavily on regional aesthetic conventions in *Oral History*. In Madden's *Bijou* the Hutchfield family also preserves close ties with the rural Appalachian past, though the generation on which Madden focuses is already established in the urban setting.

If the problems of characters who are not yet acclimated to the urban setting continue to fascinate, the existence of a recent past very different from the present also continues to be a resource for southern writers. Alex Haley draws on an Antebellum and Reconstruction history which still has relevance for contemporary southerners. Harry Crews' retracing of his poor-white origins in *A Childhood* reflects an attitude toward the past that carries over into his fiction, for Crews' protagonists are influenced by the psychological violence of their upbringing and culture. The "soft," spiritually indifferent lifestyle that Crews appears to associate with the suburban middle class is rarely more than a generation or a few miles removed from the harsh struggle for existence of the poor whites, a struggle that nonetheless many suburbanites return to in disguised forms of competition or in moments of violence. In the same vein James Dickey in *Deliverance* thrusts his crew of suburban professionals into the harsh conditions of a previous generation by transporting them to the mountain wilderness of north Georgia.

A similar assault on bourgeois sensibility, and on the dependence on technology and social organization that underpins bourgeois existence, appears in Cormac McCarthy's *The Orchard Keeper* and

Child of God, novels that detail an impoverished and uneducated white society that still exists on the underside of many southern cities. By drawing on this fertile subject, McCarthy suggests that postwar development has been superficial, for this progress has not extended to all in the New South. Also, despite its elemental qualities of violence and instinct, McCarthy's depiction of the poor white suggests an intact identity and connection with physical reality lacking in the new suburban lifestyle. More recently McCarthy has moved to the Southwest and begun to write about this region, though with the same focus on psychological violence that one finds in his treatments of the South. One should perhaps note that McCarthy's "southwest" is populated by southern immigrants and culturally is shaped by its historical connections with the South.

Perhaps more typical of recent southern fiction, however, Anne Tyler and Richard Ford write in ways that connect with mainstream American culture. In subject and style, both novelists retains elements of the southern aesthetic, yet both have moved closer to the mainstream of national concerns than had Faulkner or O'Connor, or has Styron or Percy. The treatment of mechanization in the fiction of Tyler and Ford is only slightly distinguishable from that in American fiction generally. In *A Piece of My Heart*, *Rock Springs* and other works, Richard Ford's "southerners" are expatriate, wandering outside the region, with only momentary conscious recognition of their southern past intruding in the form of a sense of radical individualism and an ethical seriousness. Ford's protagonists are indeed troubled by the absence of a coherent connection with the past and by the lack of even any sense that individual identity matters, yet most of the time they seek relief from the oppressive (and very much southern) need to make sense of society and history. Even as they probe this need further, Ford's alienated narrators find relief from their past through travel and anonymity.

Likewise, though her biographical origins are southern, Anne Tyler's characters are border-South and urban and only by a positive emphasis on family and social ritual do they show a connection with southern fictional traditions. Nonetheless, to a degree both Tyler and

Ford may be energized by a sense of connection with the southern aesthetic of fiction: there are elements of local color in Tyler's extended families which include more than their share of eccentrics and humorous naifs, while Ford's fiction, with its dramatized lack of familial and communal ties, its minimalist tone of desolation, and its recording of the loneliness of individualism, implies by its absence a traditional web of social relationships characteristic of the southern past. If the southern locale and peculiar cultural values are increasingly dropping out of southern fiction, perhaps new values are evolving which are not entirely severed from the past culture. A New South savviness and optimism moderated by a southern awareness of its place in history typifies many contemporary southern writers. The obverse, a jadedness and despair that seem to accompany the region's disillusionment with its new prosperity, may also be detected. Whatever the direction of its fiction in the nineties, certainly the southern fascination with its own history of modernization and change is a topic that has not been, and is not soon to be, exhausted.

Selected Bibliography

Anderson, Bernhard W. *Understanding the Old Testament*. 4th ed. Englewood Cliffs, N. J.: Prentice-Hall, 1986.

Andrews, William L. "'We Ain't Going Back There': The Idea of Progress in The Autobiography of Miss Jane Pittman." *Black American Literature Forum* 11 (Winter 1977): 146-49.

Arendt, Hannah. *The Human Condition*. Chicago: U of Chicago P, 1958.

Aubert, Alvin. "Ernest J. Gaines's Truly Tragic Mulatto." *Callaloo* 1(May 1978): 68-75.

Barth, J. Robert. "Faulkner and the Calvinist Tradition." *Religious Perspectives in Faulkner's Fiction*. Notre Dame: U of Notre Dame P, 1972. 11-31.

Blotner, Joseph L. *Faulkner: A Biography*. New York: Random House, 1966.

Brooks, Cleanth. "Faulkner as Poet." *Southern Literary Journal* 1 (Dec. 1968): 5-19.

Bryant, Jerry H. "Ernest J. Gaines: Change, Growth, and History." *Southern Review* 10 (October 1974): 851-64.

Carlson, Thomas M. "Flannery O'Connor: the Manichean Dilemma." *Sewanee Review* 77 (1969): 254-76.

Cobb, James C. *Industrialization and Southern Society, 1877- 1984*. Lexington: U of Kentucky P, 1984.

Cobb, James C. and Michael V. Namorato, eds. *The New Deal and the South*. Jackson: U of Mississippi P, 1984.

Cobb, James C. *The Selling of the South: The Southern Crusade for Industrial Development 1936-1980*. Baton Rouge: Louisiana State UP, 1982.

Crews, Harry. *A Childhood: The Biography of a Place*. Boston: G. K. Hall, 1979.

_____. *The Hawk Is Dying*. New York, Knopf, 1973.

Davidson, Donald. *Poems, 1922-1961*. Minneapolis: U of Minnesota P, 1968.

_____. *The Southern Writer in the Modern World*. Athens: U of Georgia P, 1958.

Duncan, Todd. "Scene and Life Cycle in Ernest Gaines' Bloodline." *Callaloo* 1 (May 1978): 85-101.

Ellul, Jacques. *Technological Society*. New York: Random House, 1967.

Fabre, Michel. "Bayonne or the Yoknapatawpha of Ernest Gaines." *Callaloo* 1 (May 1978): 110-24.

Fain, John Tyree, and Thomas Daniel Young. *The Literary Correspondence of Donald Davidson and Allen Tate*. Athens: U Georgia P, 1974.

Falkner, Murray. *The Faulkners of Mississippi*. Baton Rouge: Louisiana State UP, 1967.

Faulkner, William. *Collected Stories*. New York: Random House, 1950.

_____. *Essays, Speeches and Public Letters*. Ed. James B. Meriwether. New York: Random House, 1965.

_____. *Mosquitoes*. New York: Boni and Liveright, 1927.

_____. *New Orleans Sketches*. Ed. Carvel Collins. New York: Random House, 1958.

_____. *Pylon*. New York: Harrison Smith and Robert Hass, 1935.

_____. *Soldiers' Pay*. New York: Signet, 1968.

_____. *The Sound and the Fury*. New York: Random House, 1964.

Franklin, John Hope, and Alfred A. Moss, Jr. *From Slavery to Freedom: A History of Negro Americans*. 6th ed. New York: Knopf, 1988.

Gaines, Ernest J. *Bloodline*. New York: Dial Press, 1968.

_____. *Catherine Carmier*. New York: Atheneum, 1964.

_____. *In My Father's House*. New York: Knopf, 1978.

_____. *Of Love and Dust*. New York: Norton, 1967.

Guereschi, Edward. "Ritual and Myth in William Faulkner's *Pylon*." *Thoth* 3 (Spring 1962): 101-10.

Hardy, John Edward. *The Fiction of Walker Percy*. Urbana: U of Illilnois P, 1987.

Hassan, Ihab. "The Novel of Outrage: A Minority Voice in Postwar American Fiction." *American Scholar* 34 (1965): 239-53.

Hepburn, Kenneth W."Faulkner's *Mosquitoes*: A Poetic Turning Point." *Twentieth Century Literature* 17 (1971): 19-28.

Humphreys, Josephine. *Rich in Love*. New York: Penguin, 1988.

Kawin, Bruce. *Faulkner and Film*. New York: Ungar, 1977.

Irwin, John T. *Doubling and Incest/Repetition and Revenge: A Speculative Reading of Faulkner*. Baltimore: Johns Hopkins U P, 1975.

Katz, Claire. "Flannery O'Connor's Rage of Vision." *American Literature* 46 (1974): 54-67.

Keller, Jane C. "The Figures of the Empiricist and the Rationalist the Fiction of Flannery O'Connor." *Arizona Quarterly* 28 (1972): 263-73.

Kinney, Arthur F. *Flannery O'Connor's Library: Resources for Being*. Athens: U of Georgia P, 1985.

Lawson, Lewis. "Walker Percy's Indirect Communications." *Texas Studies in Language and Literature* 11 (1969): 867-900.

Leary, Lewis. *Southern Excursions: Essays on Mark Twain and Others.* Baton Rouge: Louisiana State U P, 1971.

MacMillan, Duane. "*Pylon*: From Short Stories to Major Work." *Mosiac* 7 (Fall 1973): 185-212.

Maritain, Jacques. *Art and Scholasticism with Other Essays.* Trans. J. Scanlan. New York: Scribner's, 1930.

Marx, Leo. *The Machine and the Garden: Technology and the Pastoral Ideal in America.* New York: Oxford U P, 1964.

Mencken, H. L. *Prejudices: Second Series.* New York: Knopf, 1920.

Millgate, Michael. "Faulkner and the Air: The Background of *Pylon.*" *Michigan Quarterly Review* 3 (1964): 271-77.

Morrison, Toni. *Beloved.* New York: Knopf, 1987.

O'Brien, Michael. *The Idea of the American South: 1920- 1941.* Baltimore: Johns Hopkins U P, 1979.

O'Connor, Flannery. *The Presence of Grace, and Other Book Reviews.* Ed. Carter W. Martin. Athens: U of Georgia P, 1983.

_____. *The Habit of Being: Letters of Flannery O'Connor.* Ed. Sally Fitzgerald. New York: Farrar, Straus and Giroux, 1979.

_____. *Mystery and Manners: Occasional Prose.* Eds. Sally and Robert Fitzgerald. New York: Farrar, Straus, and Giroux, 1969.

_____. *The Complete Stories.* New York: Farrar, Straus, and Giroux, 1972.

Orwell, George. *My Country Right or Left: 1940-1943*. Ed. Sonia Orwell and Ian Angus. New York: Harcourt, Brace, Jovanovich, 1968.

Percy, Walker. *Lancelot*. New York: Farrar, Straus, and Giroux, 1977.

_____. *The Last Gentleman*. New York, Farrar, Straus, and Giroux, 1969.

_____. *Lost in the Cosmos: The Last Self-Help Book*. New York: Farrar, Straus, and Giroux, 1983.

_____. *The Thanatos Syndrome*. New York: Farrar, Straus, and Giroux, 1987.

Ransom, John Crowe. *God Without Thunder*. New York: Harcourt, Brace, 1930.

Reed, Ishmael. *Shrovetide in Old New Orleans*. Garden City, N. Y.: Doubleday, 1978.

Roskies, David G., Ed. *The Literature of Destruction: Jewish Responses to Catastrophe*. New York: Jewish Publication   . . . . Society, 1989.

Rowell, Charles H. "The Quarters: Ernest Gaines and the Sense of Place." *Southern Review* 21 (1985): 733-50.

_____. "'This Louisiana Thing That Drives Me': An Interview with Ernest J. Gaines." *Callaloo* 1 (May 1978): 39-51.

Rubin, Louis D, Jr. "Flannery O'Connor and the Bible Belt." *The Added Dimension: The Art and Mind of Flannery O'Connor*. Eds. Melvin J. Friedman and Lewis A. Lawson. New York: Fordham UP, 1966: 49-72.

_____. *The Wary Fugitives: Four Poets and the South*. Baton Rouge: Louisiana State UP, 1978.

Shelton, Frank. "*In My Father's House*: Ernest Gaines After Jane Pittman." *Southern Review* 17 (1981): 340-45.

Simpson, Lewis P. *The Dispossessed Garden*. Athens: U of Georgia P, 1975.

_____. *The Man of Letters in New England and the South*. Baton Rouge: Louisiana State U P, 1973.

Singal, Daniel Joseph. *The War Within: From Victorian to Modernist Thought in the South, 1919-1945*. Chapel Hill: U of North Carolina P, 1982.

Slatoff, Walter J. *Quest for Failure: A Study of William Faulkner*. Ithaca: Cornell U P, 1960.

Smythe, Mabel M., Ed. *The Black American Reference Book*. Englewood Cliffs, N. J.: Prentice-Hall, 1976.

Squires, Radcliffe. *Allen Tate: A Literary Biography*. New York: Pegasus, 1971.

_____."Will and Vision: Allen Tate's Terza Rima Poems." *Sewanee Review* 78 (1970):543-62.

Stewart, John L. *The Burden of Time*. Princeton: Princeton UP, 1965.

Styron, William. *The Confessions of Nat Turner*. New York: Signet, 1968.

_____. *The Long March*. New York: Random House, 1952.

_____. *Set This House on Fire*. New York: Bantam, 1981.

_____. *Sophie's Choice*. New York: Bantam, 1980.

Tate, Allen. *Collected Essays*. Denver: Swallow, 1959.

_____. *Collected Poems, 1919-1976*. New York: Farrar, Straus and Giroux, 1977.

_____."A Distinguished Poet." *Hound and Horn* 3 (Summer 1930): 582-83.

_____. *Essays of Four Decades*. Chicago: Swallow, 1968.

_____. *Mr. Pope and Other Poems*. New York: Minton, Balch, 1928.

_____. *Reason in Madness: Critical Essays*. New York: G. P. Putnam's, 1941.

Tindall, George Brown. *The Emergence of the New South, 1913-1945*. Baton Rouge: Louisiana State UP, 1967.

Torchiana, Donald. "Faulkner's *Pylon* and the Structure of Modernity." *Modern Fiction Studies* 3 (1957): 291-308.

Tyler, Anne. *The Accidental Tourist*. New York: Knopf, 1985.

_____. *Dinner at the Homesick Restaurant*. New York: Knopf, 1982.

_____. *A Slipping-Down Life*. New York: Knopf, 1970.

Utter, Glenn H. "The Individual in Technological Society: Walker Percy's *Lancelot*." *Journal of Popular Culture* (1982): 121-30.

Walker, Alice. *The Color Purple*. New York: Harcourt, Brace, Jovanovich, 1982.

_____. *Good Night, Willie Lee, I'll See You in the Morning: Poems*. New York: Dial, 1979.

_____. *Horses Make a Landscape More Beautiful*. New York: Harcourt, Brace, Jovanovich, 1984.

_____. *Living By the Word: Selected Writings, 1973- 1987*. Harcourt, Brace, Jovanovich, 1988.

Wideman, John. "*Of Love and Dust*: A Reconsideration." *Callaloo* 1 (May 1978): 76-84.

Woodward, C. Vann. *Origins of the New South, 1877-1913*. Baton Rouge: Louisiana State UP, 1951.

Wright, Gavin. *Old South, New South: Revolutions in the Southern Economy Since the Civil War*. New York: Basic Books, 1986.

Wyatt-Brown, Bertram. *Southern Honor: Ethics and Behavior in the Old South*. New York: Oxford U P, 1982.

Worcester Polytechnic Institute
Studies in Science, Technology and Culture

Worcester Polytechnic Institute Studies in Science, Technology, and Culture aims to publish monographs, tightly-edited collections of essays, and research tools in interdisciplinary topics which investigate the relationships of science and technology to social and cultural issues and impacts. The series is edited by Lance Schachterle (Chair, Division of Interdisciplinary Affairs and Professor of English, WPI) and Francis C. Lutz (Associate Dean for Projects and Professor of Civil Engineering, WPI). The editors invite proposals in English from beginning and established scholars throughout the world whose research interests focus on how science or technology affects the structure, values, quality, or management of our society. The series complements WPI's commitment to interdisciplinary education by providing opportunities to publish on the widest possible diversity of themes at the intersection of science, technology and culture.